AF479947

Shores of Gold
An Ode to Fife, Scotland

Text and illustrations copyright © 2024 Amy Selstad

Hardcover: ISBN 979-8-218-97638-5
Printed in the United States of America
amyselstad.com

SHORES OF GOLD

AN ODE TO FIFE, SCOTLAND

BY AMY SELSTAD

Look east of Scotland, beyond the woodlands and hills,
to a sunny peninsula known as Fife.

1

First, you'll see the Dunfermline Abbey and Palace, the final resting place of many medieval kings and queens of Scotland.

Under the pillars, you may walk by the vault of King Robert the Bruce, who led his country to victory in the Scottish War of Independence.

If you head up Northeast, you can visit the Falkland Palace and Gardens and walk in the same place as Mary Queen of Scots!

5

And just a little further north, you'll reach the shores of St Andrews, where Prince William and Princess Kate first met.

You can also spot the St Andrews Castle over there,
amidst the beachgrass swaying in the wind.

The coast of Fife has many fishing villages,
with colorful boats going up and down the waves.

King James VI once praised the coast:
"A beggar's mantle fringed wi' gold."

The fishing fleets in Fife made a huge profit from the fish that swam
in the Northern Sea. Each type of fish was unique and valuable.

If only King James VI tasted fish suppers' wrapped warmly in newspaper, topped with fresh salt n' sauce from Anstruther.

If you journey toward Loch Leven, you may discover
another treasure known as Scottish heather.

13

Heather is not only a symbol of luck in Scotland, but also a source of nectar and pollen for bees!

If you're up for a longer walk, consider taking the Fife Coastal Path. It offers beautiful views of the ocean and the shoreline is full of cool rock formations.

In St Andrews, you can stroll along the Lade Braes path,
where the shimmering water is lined with elm trees.

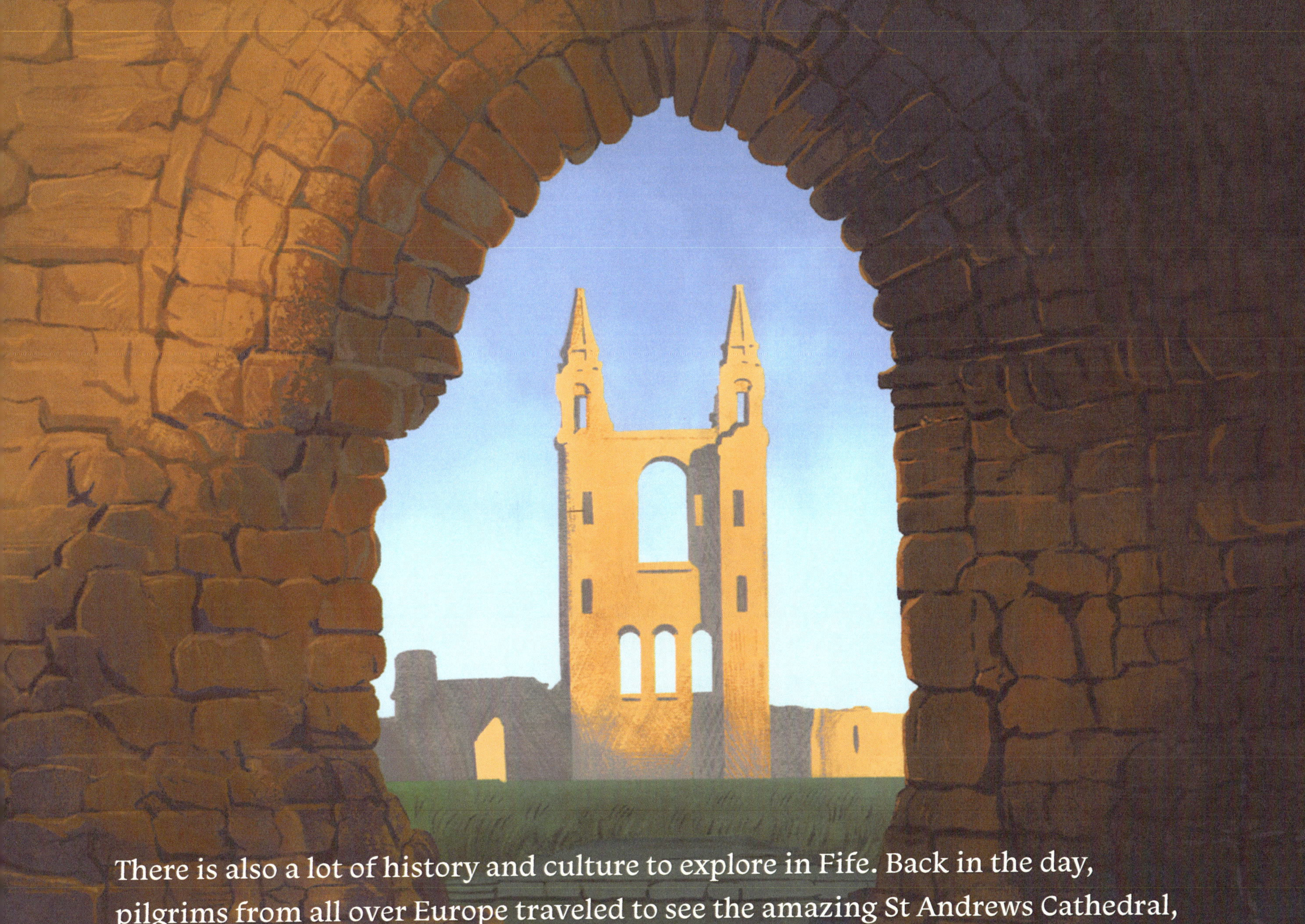

There is also a lot of history and culture to explore in Fife. Back in the day, pilgrims from all over Europe traveled to see the amazing St Andrews Cathedral, which was considered a national shrine.

However, today most people visit St Andrews to golf. After all, it is home to the world's oldest golf course and is the birthplace of the sport!

If you do visit Fife, you'll learn that Fifers are some
of the kindest people you will ever meet.

20

With trays of teacups and shortbread and spoonfuls
of strawberry crumble, they are very hospitable.

They're happy to share the fruits of their labor
with their neighbors, often giving away fresh
produce from their gardens.

Saint Margaret, who ruled as Queen in Fife,
was known for her kindness and charity.
Every day, she fed the poor before she ate.

As you say your goodbyes, don't forget the memories of fishing boats, castles, and wonderful people you met. And who knows, you might end up planning another visit to Fife soon!

Author's Note

One day, I wrote a poem about a county in Scotland called Fife. For seven months, I lived, explored, and grew to appreciate the nature there. Then, I moved back home and wrote my memories into a poem. The poem, originally titled "Ode to Fife," later evolved into my first picture book, titled **Shores of Gold.** This book can be thought of as a love letter to Fife.

Places to visit

1. St Andrews
2. Anstruther
3. Crail
4. Falkland
5. Dunfermline
6. Guardbridge
7. Loch Leven
8. Tentsmuir

Ode to Fife (original poem)

Look east, beyond the Lomond hills,
to the sun-rimmed peninsula:
fair-faced for a pillared palace
for Scots to honor their kings.
The memory of monarchy
living in Fife.
There, in the forests of Falkland
where Mary Stuart breathed and walked.
There, in the sands of St Andrews,
where royal children played and grew.
And there, in the wind-swept beachgrass,
stood a castle too.

Every season, the shores are full;
more treasure fills the fisher's net
than any king or queen could hold.
King James himself praised the coast:
"a beggar's mantle fringed wi gold."
(The harbor's gold)
fish of the Northern Sea, whether
haddock, salmon, cod, or hake.
If only he tasted fish and chips
wrapped warmly in torn newspaper,
topped with fresh salt and vinegar
from Anstruther.

There's more gold hidden in the moors,
where yellow flowers poke freckles
on bushes and bees make honey
from heather: Scotland's sweet nectar
and more treasure on the shore
where seagulls soar.
April bluebells and daffodils
line the creek in Lade Braes,
where ducklings follow their mother
to bathe in fresh water with trees
providing shade. It was here
the pilgrims prayed.

The people of Fife inherit
this heavenly land and open
their doors to weary wanderers.
With trays of teacups and shortbread
and spoonfuls of rhubarb crumble,
they are humble.
The heart of many Fifers learned
to give as their homeland gave:
with bountiful love and beauty,
seeds first sown with holy hands
to give those who tread alone
a taste of their home.

Nin Brudermann

Twelve O'Clock In London: Austria/Autriche

Inhalt

Contents

Twelve O'Clock in London World Map, 2010, mixed media collage on paper, 72 x 90 x 4 inch
(detail), exhibition view Kunstraum Dornbirn, photo: Robert Fessler

Anna Karina Hofbauer

Vom Spielen mit der Realität

Mit hoher Geschwindigkeit nähern sich zwei schwarze Hubschrauber der Dachterrasse einer Wohnung nahe dem East River in Brooklyn, New York, worauf sich Nin Brudermann befindet. Es ist kurz nach 9/11 und jegliche außergewöhnlichen Veränderungen im Luftraum werden von der Homeland Security der US-Behörde beobachtet. Der Anlass des Anflugs der Hubschrauber war ein Wetterballon, der zwar an einer Fischerleine fixiert war, der aber nichtsdestotrotz eine Höhe erreicht hatte, die in den Augen der Behörde schon zu hoch war und dadurch eine potenzielle Bedrohung der nationalen Sicherheit darstellte. Die Künstlerin signalisierte den Piloten sofort, dass sie das Unterfangen unterbrechen würde. Die Fischerleine samt Wetterballon wurde eingerollt und die Hubschrauber drehten wieder ab. Dies war der erste Versuch Brudermanns, einen eigenen Wetterballon von ihrem Zuhause aus zu starten, nachdem sie von ihrer Expedition auf der Isla de Vieques, eine Insel in der Karibik nahe Puerto Rico, dementsprechend dem Amerikanischen Commonwealth zugehörig, zurückgekehrt war.

Das Projekt *NASD Projekt Fledermaus* hatte die Künstlerin in diese Gegend geführt, wo sie auf das Phänomen der Wetterballons aufmerksam gemacht worden war. So wurde ein neues Projekt geboren und Brudermann begann zu recherchieren: Das Steigenlassen der Wetterballons stellte sich als ein einzigartiges, zugleich jedoch als ein weitgehend unbekanntes tägliches Ritual der Vereinten Nationen heraus. Es wird von der WMO (World Meteorological Organization), die in Genf ihre Hauptzentrale hat, dirigiert und die Ergebnisse und die Daten der einzelnen Wetterstationen werden dort zusammengeführt. Jeden Tag, in jedem Land unseres Planeten lassen Meteorologen um 00:00 Uhr und 12:00 Uhr Londoner Zeit Wetterballons in den Himmel steigen. Der Wetterballon, der meistens aus Gummi oder Latex besteht, wird von den Meteorologen, mit Messgeräten und speziellen Radiosonden ausgestattet, in die Stratosphäre losgeschickt, um Daten über Temperatur, Luftdruck und Feuchtigkeit zu registrieren. In seiner Lebenszeit erreicht ein Wetterballon eine Höhe von 20 bis 30 Kilometer, wobei er mit zunehmender Höhe und nachlassendem Luftdruck beginnt, sich bis über zwölf Meter auszudehnen, bevor er dann endgültig zerplatzt. Vor seinem Zerplatzen kann man mit einem guten Auge oder mit den entsprechenden optischen Hilfsmitteln das fantastische Ereignis der Ausdehnung des Ballons beobachten. Die Reste des

Anna Karina Hofbauer

Playing with Reality

At high speed, two black helicopters approached the roof terrace of an apartment close to the East River in Brooklyn, on which Nin Brudermann stood. It was not long after 9/11 and any unusual changes in airspace was under observation by US Homeland Security. The reason for the helicopters' approach was a weather balloon affixed to a fishing line that had nonetheless reached a height that in the eyes of the Homeland authority was too high and thus a potential threat to national security. The artist immediately signaled the pilots that she was breaking off the operation. The fishing line and weather balloon were rolled up, and the helicopters turned away. This was Brudermann's first attempt to send off her own weather balloon from her home, after she had returned from the Isla de Vieques, an island near Puerto Rico and thus part of the American commonwealth.

The *NASD Projekt Fledermaus* (Bat Project) had led the artist to this island, where she was made aware of the phenomenon of weather balloons. Thus a new project was born and Brudermann began to do research on the significance of weather balloons, which turned out to be a unique, yet, at the same time, a generally unknown daily ritual of the United Nations. The daily flight of weather balloons is directed by the WMO (World Meteorological Organization), whose headquarters in Geneva brings together the results and the data from the individual weather stations. Every day in every country on our planet, meteorologists send weather balloons into the sky at 00:00 and 12:00 London time. The meteorologists equip the weather balloons, mostly made of rubber or latex, with gauges and special radiosondes and send them into the stratosphere to measure and register data on temperature, air pressure and humidity. In its lifetime, a weather balloon reaches a height of 20 to 30 kilometers where, from a rising height and reduced air pressure, it begins to expand to up to twelve meters before it finally bursts. Before it bursts, a sharp eye (or one aided by a corresponding optical device) can watch the fantastic event of the balloon's expansion. The remains of the balloon and its equipment fall back to earth via a small parachute. Most radiosondes have an integrated GPS tracker, so that the device can be found. The large amount of information is transmitted by radio to the respective meteorological stations. The Norwegian

Ballons und die Geräte kehren mithilfe eines kleinen Fallschirms zum Boden zurück. Die meisten Radiosonden haben einen integrierten GPS-Tracker, damit man das Gerät wiederfinden kann. Die vielen Informationen werden per Funk an die jeweilige meteorologische Station gesendet. Die erste Einladung, einen Wetterballon gemeinsam mit Meteorologen steigen zu lassen, kam von der norwegischen Luftwaffe, die Brudermann mitnahm zu der im Arktischen Ozean gelegenen norwegischen Insel Jan Mayen, ein sogenannter Hot Spot, dessen Daten rar sind. Danach war Brudermann zwei Monate mit einem Eisbrecher in Australien unterwegs, um aus der Antarktis einen Wetterballon steigen zu lassen. Dieser wurde häufig unter schwierigen Wetterbedingungen vom Schiff aus in die Stratosphäre hoch gelassen. An diese Wetterballons, die sie selbst losschickte, befestigte die Künstlerin eine Kamera, die per Funk die Bilder der oberen Sphären zu ihrem Computer zurücksendete. Diese Observationen, die das eigentliche Interesse Brudermanns sind, nennen sich „Upper Air Observations". Unter anderem startete Thomas Jefferson diese Art der Untersuchungen und schrieb im Jahre 1784 von der meteorologischen Verwendung der Ballons. Seine Versuche und Beobachtungen konnten ein neues Licht auf das Thermometer, Barometer, Hygrometer sowie auf Regen, Schnee, Hagel und andere Phänomene werfen, welche die Atmosphäre als ihr Theater verwendeten, so Jefferson. Das Wet-

terballonprojekt erwies sich bald für Brudermann als ein weltumspannendes Unterfangen. Da sie nicht überall hinreisen konnte, fing sie an, die einzelnen meteorologischen Stationen anzuschreiben, mit der Bitte, ihre Forschungen zu unterstützen. Zahlreiche Staaten wie zum Beispiel der Iran und Chile beteiligten sich aktiv am Projekt, was bedeutete, dass Meteorologen aus den verschiedensten Ländern nach den Anweisungen von Brudermann die Wetterballonroutine filmten, um die Aufnahmen anschließend der Künstlerin zu senden. Die meisten dieser Videos bestehen hauptsächlich aus statischen Bildern, die von den einzelnen Wetterstationen stammen und vereinzelt aus persönlichen Aufnahmen von den Meteorologen selbst, die individuelle Perspektiven der wissenschaftlichen Routine zeigen.

Als großflächige Projektion wird die aus den vielen einzelnen Aufnahmen zu einer digitalen Collage erstellte Zusammenschau im Kunstraum Dornbirn arrangiert. So schafft Nin Brudermann das Unfassbare – ein ultimatives völkerverbindendes Projekt, das alle Landesgrenzen und Feindschaften temporär überwindet. Die zahlreichen Projektionen, die wie ein einheitliches momentanes Bild erscheinen, sind Zeugnisse, die eine schon dagewesene Realität repräsentieren. Zusammengestellt verweisen die Videos auf Momente, die einzelnen Protogonisten zugeschrieben werden können – jedes Video hat seine eigene Geschichte, jedes liefert seinen eigenen Verweis

air force was the first to invite Brudermann, together with meteorologists, to send up a weather balloon, which Brudermann took with her to the Norwegian Jan Mayen Island in the Artic Ocean, a so-called hot spot, a site whose data are rare. Following which Brudermann was two months with an icebreaker in Australia in order to release a weather balloon from Antarctica. This was often sent aloft into the stratosphere from the ship itself under difficult weather conditions. The artist attached a camera to these weather balloons that she herself released, which sent pictures of the upper spheres back to her computer by radio. These observations, which are the actual focus of Brudermann's interest, are called "upper air observations". Thomas Jefferson, among others, began with this kind of investigation and in 1784 wrote about the meteorological use of balloons. Such studies, Jefferson thought, could throw a new light on the thermometer, barometer and hygrometer, on the rain, snow, hail and other phenomena, which the atmosphere uses as its stage. Brudermann's weather balloon project soon proved to be a world-embracing undertaking. Since she couldn't travel any and everywhere, she began to write to the individual meteorological stations to request their participation. Thus many countries, e.g., Iran and Chile, took an active part in the project, which meant that meteorologists in the relevant countries

filmed the weather-balloon routine according to Brudermann's instructions and finished by sending the results to the artist. Most of the videos consisted mainly of static images from single weather stations and infrequently of the individual films mostly shot by the meteorologists themselves and thus show individual perspectives of the scientific routine.

Together these videos constitute a large-scale projection in Kunstraum Dornbirn made up of a digital collage of many single shots. She has thus achieved the inconceivable: an unsurpassed people-linking project that overcomes all national boundaries and animosities, at least temporarily. The many projections that appear like a uniform, momentary picture are, however, testimony to a reality that represents the reality of what has been. Assembled together, the videos point to the factors that can be assigned to individual protagonists: each has its own history, each its own reference to that decisive moment. Thus an unparalleled correspondence developed, the results of which can be found in the exhibition as pieces of evidence. Different cords and ropes in very different materials and colors have been fixed to Kunstraum Dornbirn's protruding iron girders and function like walls from where the material – such as letters, photos, a camera, video tapes and antenna – are attached to the suspended transparent walls. Together they generate a multiplex and interesting

auf den entscheidenden Moment des Ballosteigenlassens. So entwickelte sich zugleich eine einmalige Korrespondenz, deren Ergebnisse in der Ausstellung als Beweisstücke wiederzufinden sind. Unterschiedliche Schnüre und Seile in den verschiedensten Materialien und Farben sind auf den herausragenden Eisenträgern des Kunstraums Dornbirn befestigt und funktionieren wie Wände, wo das Material wie Briefe, Fotos, eine Kamera, Videobänder und Antennen an den herabhängenden transparenten Wänden befestigt ist. Zusammen erzeugen diese unterschiedlichsten Versatzstücke eine vielfältige und interessante schwebende Collage, die den Besuchern einen Einblick in die umfangreiche Korrespondenz gibt. Ergänzend befindet sich eine Weltkarte an der Wand, die den Stellenwert der mehr als neunzig aktiv teilnehmenden Weltnationen dokumentiert. Zugleich ist die Weltkarte ein Beweis für die akribische und detaillierte Arbeit Brudermanns, für ein von außen gesehen fast unmögliches Projekt. Mit kugeligen Pinnnadeln wird jedes Land markiert, und jede Farbe hat eine eigene Bedeutung. So bedeutet beispielsweise Schwarz, dass das Land entweder nicht mitmachen wollte oder technische Probleme auftraten, die die Partizipation an dem Projekt unmöglich machten. Die zahlreichen bunten schmalen Haftmarker lassen den permanenten Kommunikationsprozess sowie die alltägliche Auseinandersetzungen der Künstlerin mit den einzelnen Stationen anhand von hunderten von Kommentaren nachvollziehen. Die Weltkarte befand sich in dem Zeitraum von 2001 bis 2009 in einem ständigen Entwicklungsprozess und jedes Email, jedes Schreiben und jede Art der Kommunikation wurde auf der Karte, die auch zur Übersicht der Künstlerin diente, aufgezeichnet. Eher unauffällig platziert, befindet sich in der Collage-Installation eine eingerahmte Fotografie, auf der Brudermann zusammen mit dem UN-Generalsekretär Ban Kimoon zu sehen ist. Die Künstlerin war 2009 zur Weltklimakonferenz der WMO nach Genf eingeladen worden und stellte dort in einem performativen Akt Ban Ki-moon ihr Projekt vor. Brudermann schaffte es, dem Generalsekretär die Frage zu stellen, ob er sich bewusst wäre, welche grenzüberschreitenden Aktionen zweimal täglich einen völkerverbindenden und staatenkollaborativen Akt darstellten. Ban Kimoon musste diese Frage unbeantwortet im Raum stehen lassen, lies sich jedoch nach dieser kurzen Intervention einen Ballon von der Künstlerin signieren. Das Treffen mit dem Generalsekretär war eine Art symbolischer Schlussakt des Projektes.

Die bereits früher installierte Wetterballon-Arbeit hat sich im Kunstraum Dornbirn erweitert und eine neue Dimension gefunden. Die Performance, die denselben Titel wie die Ausstellung trägt, *Twelve O'Clock in London: Austria/Autriche*, wurde zur Vernissage uraufgeführt. Eine große blonde Frau mit einer medusaähnlichen Frisur und einem Kleid – eine Symbiose

floating collage that allows visitors a sight of the voluminous correspondence. To complete the picture, there is a world map that documents the more than ninety actively participating nations in the world. At the same time, the world map is proof of Brudermann's meticulous and detailed work, a project that, viewed from outside, seems impossible. Every country is marked with spherical pins, and each pin color has its specific meaning. Thus black means that the country either did not want to participate or that technical problems made participation in the project impossible. With the help of the many slim, colored markers and hundreds of comments, you can follow the daily struggle of the artist with the single stations in their permanent process of communication. In the period from 2001 to 2009, the world map was in a constant state of evolution, and every e-mail, every letter and every sort of communication was registered on the map that served the artist as an overview. Quite inconspicuous and more at the rear of the collaged installation, a framed photograph is found on which Brudermann can be seen together with the UN General Secretary, Ban Ki-moon. Namely in 2009 the artist was invited to Geneva to the World Climate Conference of the WMO, and in a performative act she introduced Ban Ki-moon to her project. Brudermann managed to ask the SecretaryGeneral whether he could say which border-crossing actions are performed twice every day and represent a people-bonding and nation-collaborative act. Ban Ki-moon had to leave this question unanswered but after this short intervention ordered a balloon signed by the artist. The meeting with the Secretary-General hereby symbolized and confirmed the fact that the project was concluded.

The work with weather balloons was however extended to Kunstraum Dornbirn and found a new dimension. The performance has the same title as the exhibition, *Twelve O'Clock in London: Austria/Autriche*, and had its world première at the exhibit opening. A tall blond woman with a Medusa-like hairdo and a costume that represented a symbiosis between a flight attendant and a Star Trek figure entered Kunstraum Dornbirn against the backdrop of the many projections of the daily balloon-releasing ritual, and then let the door slam behind her. She took up a position next to the table that was arranged with meteorological devices and effects and stared into the audience. She then gradually began the procedure of unrolling the weather balloon in order to fill it with helium. While this was in progress, she assembled the other necessary things and added them to the now helium-filled weather balloon and left the Kunstraum with it in hand. Once outside she released the weather balloon with reflector and parachute into the sky and afterwards retreated out of public sight.

aus einem Flugbegleiterinnen- und einem Star-Trek-Kostüm – betritt den Kunstraum Dornbirn. Im Hintergrund sind die vielen Projektionen des täglichen Wetterballon-Rituals zu sehen. Die Frau lässt die Tür hinter sich knallen, stellt sich zu dem mit meteorologischen Geräten und Effekten vorbereiteten Tisch und starrt ins Publikum. Langsam macht sie sich an die Prozedur, den Wetterballon auszurollen, um diesen schließlich mit Helium zu füllen. Währenddessen sammelt sie die restlichen benötigten Dinge, bindet diese zusammen und fügt endgültig den mit Helium befüllten Wetterballon dazu und verlässt den Kunstraum. Draußen angekommen, lässt sie den Wetterballon samt Reflektor und Fallschirm in den Himmel hoch steigen und verlässt danach das Blickfeld des Publikums.

So verkörpert die Performance Brudermanns einen bedeutenden Teil ihrer künstlerischen Arbeit und zwar das Spiel mit der Inszenierung. Die Inszenierung, die in der Performance *Twelve O'Clock in London: Austria/Autriche* als ein Zeichen des Realen zu verstehen ist, verweist auf die tatsächlichen Ereignisse, wenn die Meteorologen weltweit jeden Tag um Punkt zwölf Uhr mittags und nachts jeweils einen Wetterballon steigen lassen. Die Künstlerin schafft es mit ihrer Performance, das Konzeptuelle in eine andere Realität und zwar jene eines künstlerischen Akts zu versetzen. Die Performance spielt – bereits im Titel – mit dem Genre des Eurovision Song Con-

tests und macht daraus einen Staatencontest. Man könnte von einer Verdrehung oder Veränderung der unumgänglichen Tatsache sprechen, dass es zu einer Konzeptualisierung der Realität gekommen ist. In der Performance verwendet Brudermann die wissenschaftliche Materie als Kulisse, sozusagen als Grundlage für die Performance und im Endeffekt für die Ausstellung selbst. Die Performance, die aus dem inhaltlichen Fundus, dem meteorologischen Akt, schöpft, führt Brudermann ad absurdum und in eine konzeptuelle Sphäre hinein. Schlussendlich dient der meteorologische Akt als seriöse Untermalung eines langjährigen Projektes, dessen Bedeutung weit über ein rein ästhetisches Erlebnis hinausgeht. Die Faszination liegt vielmehr auf dem politischen Aspekt der Völkerverbindung, die jeden Tag, sogar zweimal täglich, praktiziert wird, ohne dass dies im Bewusstsein der meisten Menschen realisiert wird. Damit betreibt Brudermann ein Vexierspiel mit Kunst, Politik, Wissenschaft und Natur und führt nicht nur die Absurdität manch spezialisierter wissenschaftlicher Aktivitäten vor Augen, sondern auch deren Bedeutung. Nin Brudermann hinterfragt letztendlich das, was uns als Realität erscheint.

Anna Karina Hofbauer, Kuratorin

Thus Brudermann's performance embodied a significant part of her artistic work, to wit, her play on its theatrical staging. The dramatic production is understood to be a performance of *Twelve O'Clock in London: Austria/Autriche* as a manifestation of reality, which indicates factual events, namely that meteorologists across the world release weather balloons into the air every day on the dot of twelve noon and every night at midnight. With her performance the artist managed to translate the conceptual into another reality and did so in an artistic act. The title of the performance, and the performance itself, plays with the genre of the Eurovision Song Contest and turns it into a contest of nations. One could speak of a twist or a change to the unavoidable fact that it could come to this conceptualization of reality. In the performance, she uses the scientific material as a backdrop, i.e., a foundation for the performance and, in the end, for the exhibition. Brudermann reduces ad absurdum the performance that draws on a thematic substructure, the meteorological act, and shifts it to a conceptual domain. In the end, the meteorological act serves as an earnest accompaniment to a long-term project, whose significance goes much further than an aesthetic event. Its fascination lies much more in a political, people-uniting aspect that takes place every day and even twice daily without most people ever being aware of it. So Bruder-

mann carries on a flip-flop game with art, politics, science and nature and not only opens our eyes to the absurdity of many a specialized scientific activity, but also to its significance. What Nin Brudermann calls into question is reality as we see it.

Anna Karina Hofbauer, curator

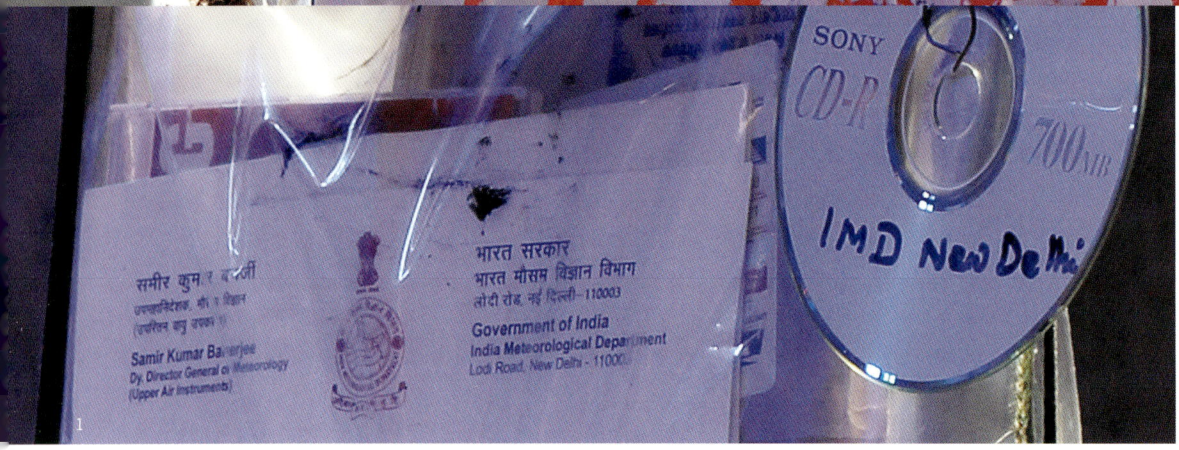

1) *Twelve O'Clock in London,* 2012, mixed media installation, dim. var., exhibition view Kunstraum Dornbirn
(details), photos: Robert Fessler 2) *Twelve O'Clock in London: Austria/Autriche,* 2012, performance Kunstraum
Dornbirn, photo: Robert Fessler

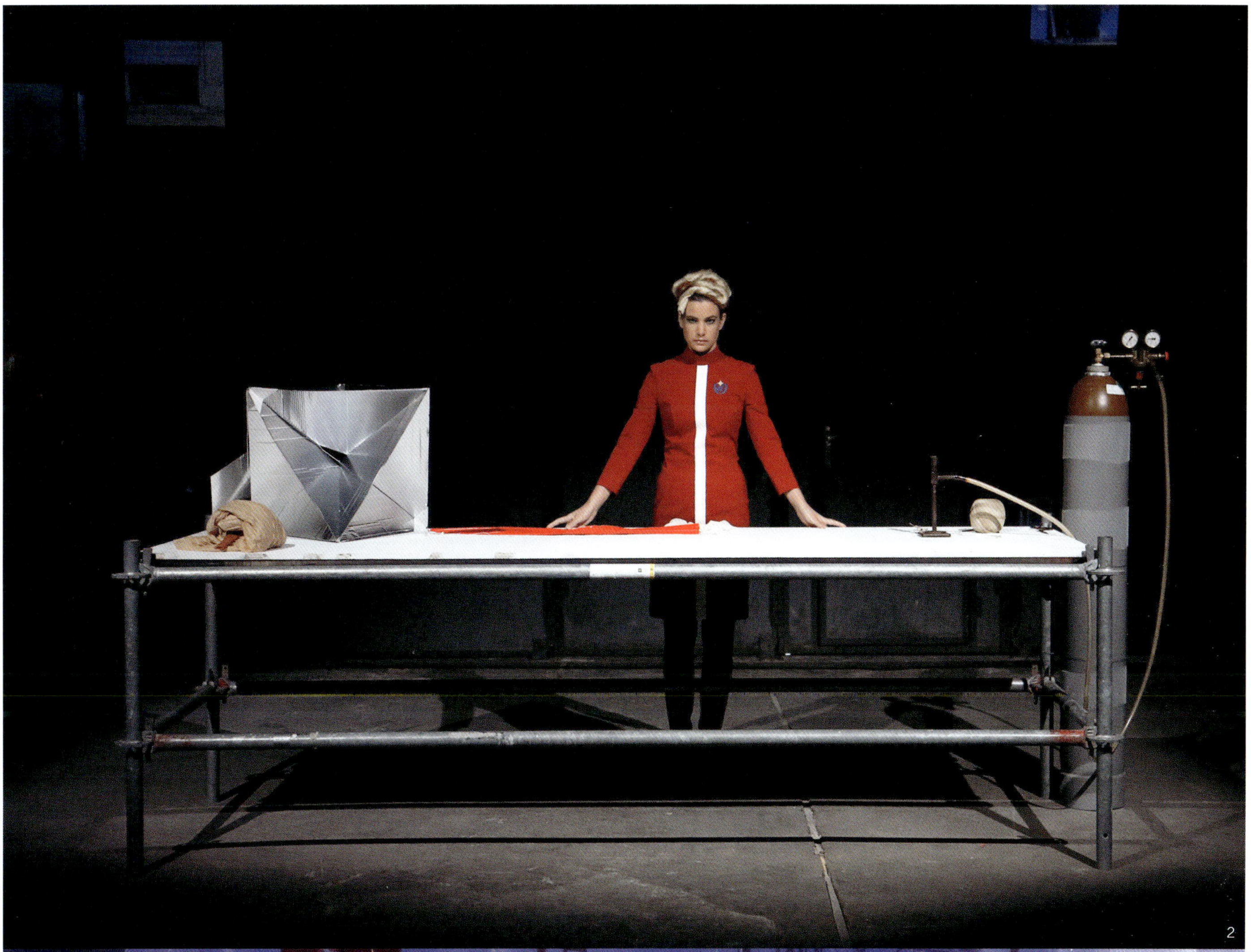
2

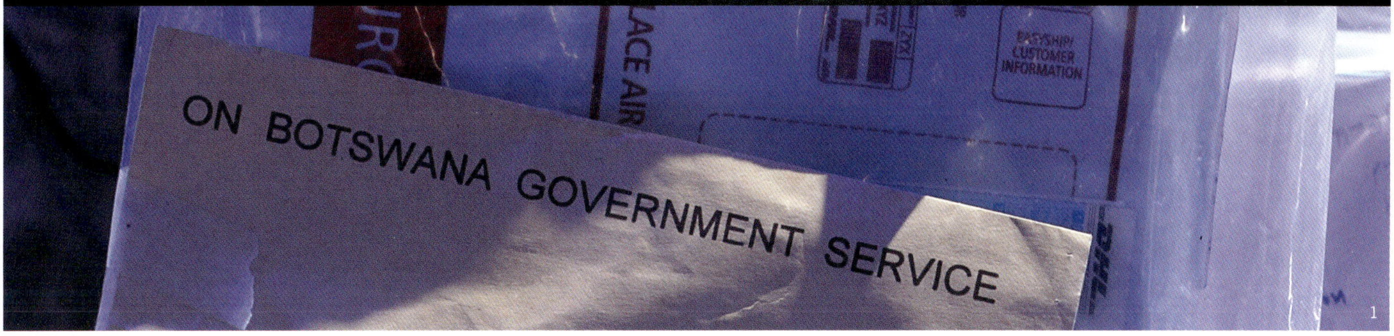
ON BOTSWANA GOVERNMENT SERVICE
EASYSHIP/
CUSTOMER
INFORMATION
1

RNMENT SERV
23.6.09
$ 003.00
POSTAGE PAID
H1123
DAGA
FROM RUSSIA,
SABRY EL
EMAIL
1

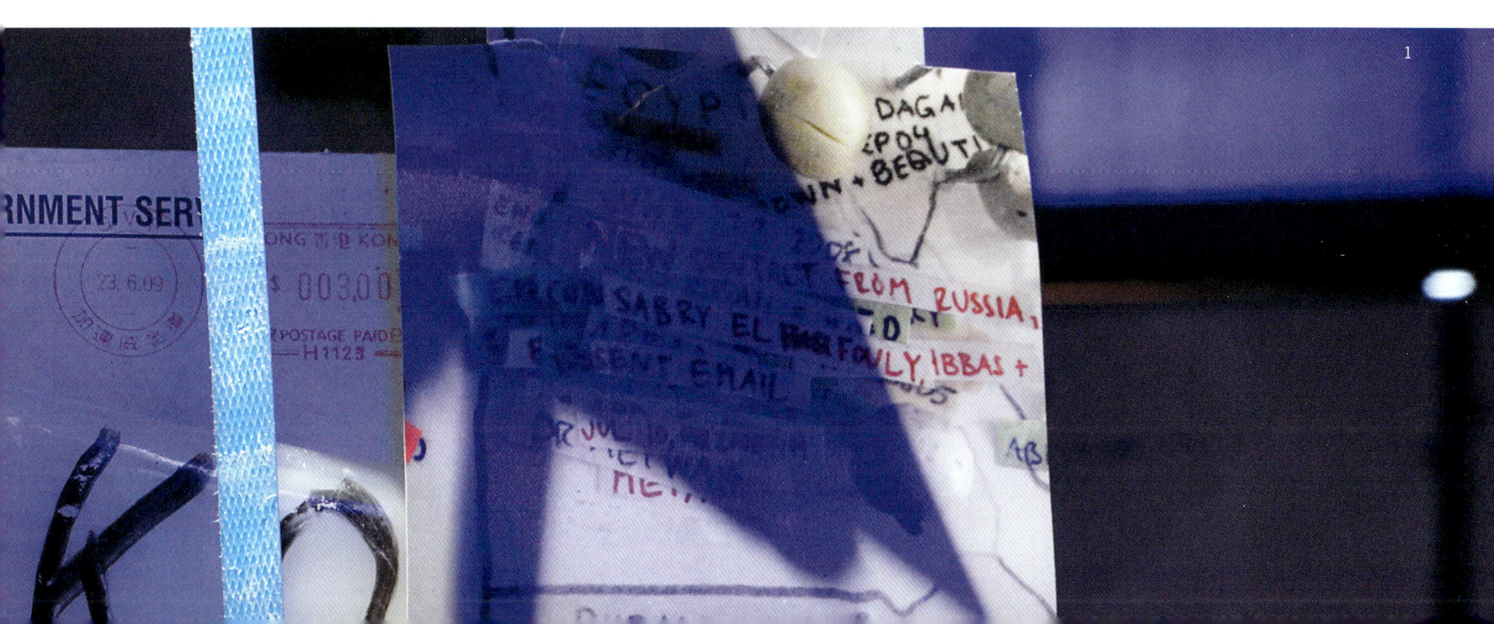

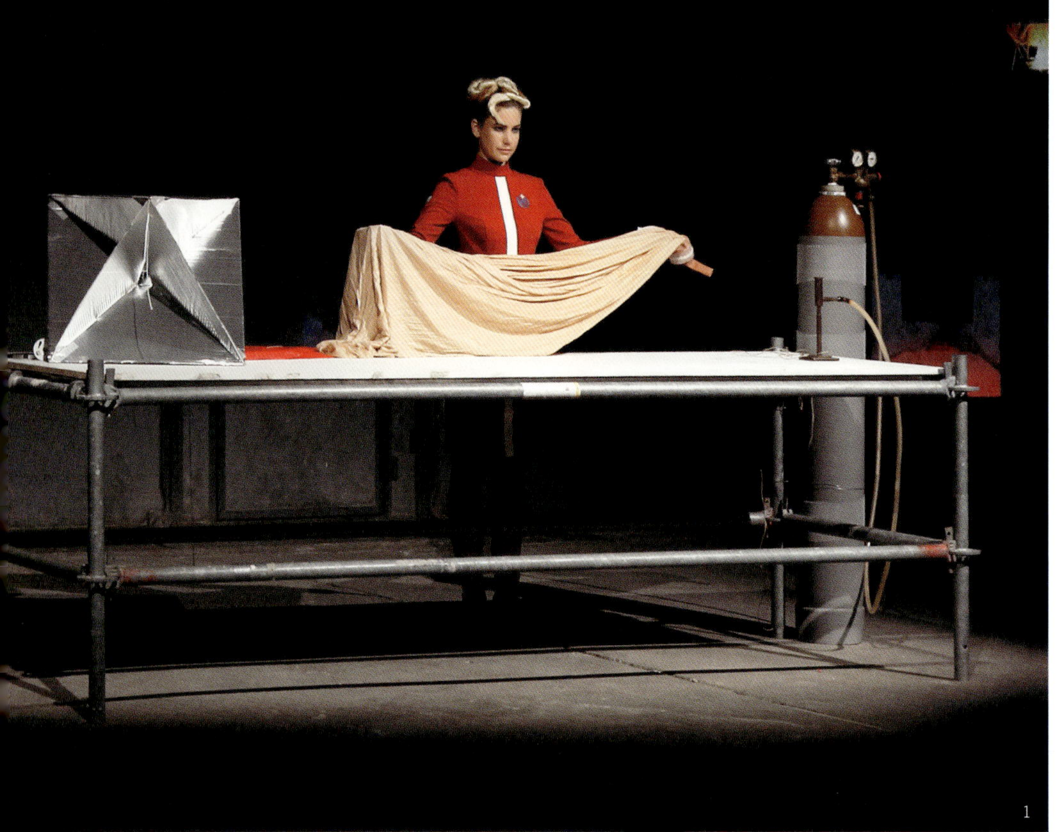

1) *Twelve O'Clock in London: Austria/Autriche,* 2012, performance Kunstraum Dornbirn, photo: Robert Fessler 2) *Twelve O'Clock in London,* 2010, 7 HD channel video installation TRT 22'00, video still United States Department of Commerce – U.S. National Ocean & Atmospheric Administration 3) *Twelve O'Clock in London,* 2010, 7 HD channel video installation TRT 22'00, video still, LR Ministry of Environment of the Republic of Latvia – Latvian Envirnoment Geology and Meteorology Agency 4) *Twelve O'Clock in London,* 2012, mixed media installation, dim. var., installation view Kunstraum Dornbirn (detail), photo: Robert Fessler

5) *Twelve O'Clock in London,* 2010, 7 HD channel video installation TRT 22'00, video stills, Performative Balloon Launch, Nin Brudermann, Venice Biennale 2003, in collaboration with Makrolab and Ministero della Difesa Repubblica Italiana – Servicio Meteorologica 6) Meteorological Instruments Météo-France, Kerguelen (F), Indian Ocean, photo: Nin Brudermann, 2002 7) *Twelve O'Clock in London World Map,* 2010, mixed media collage on paper, 72 x 90 x 4 inch (details), production phase, photos: Nin Brudermann

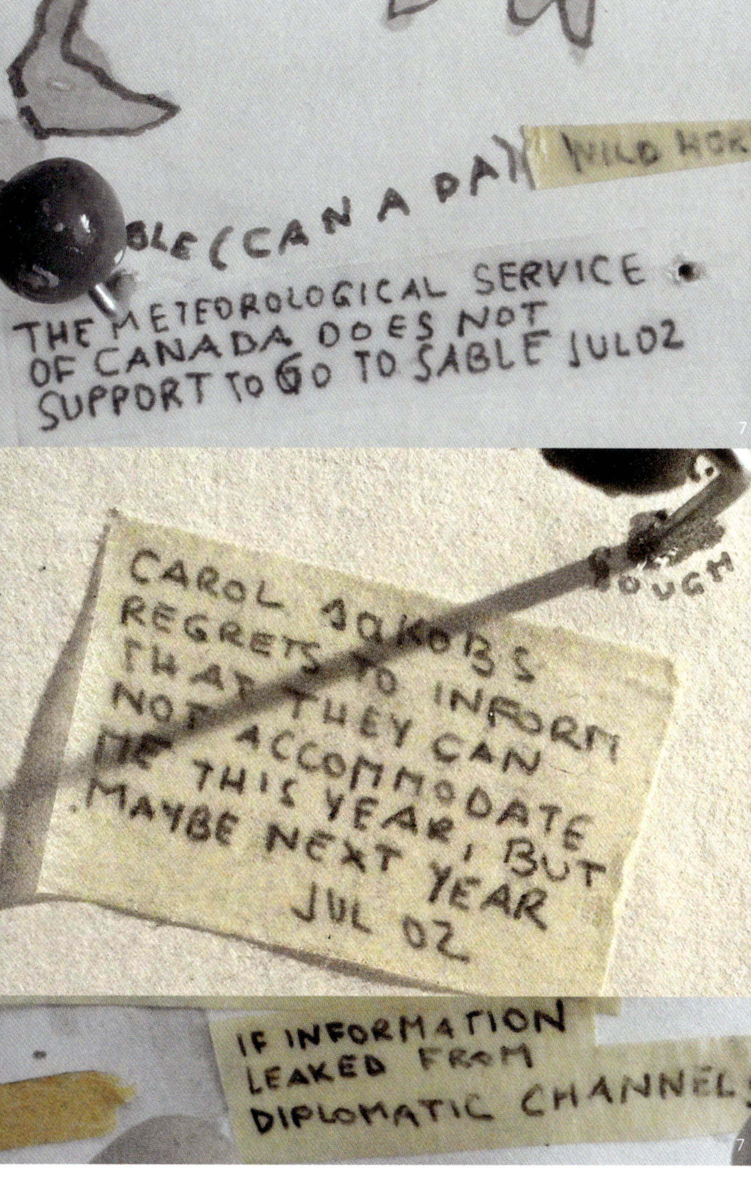

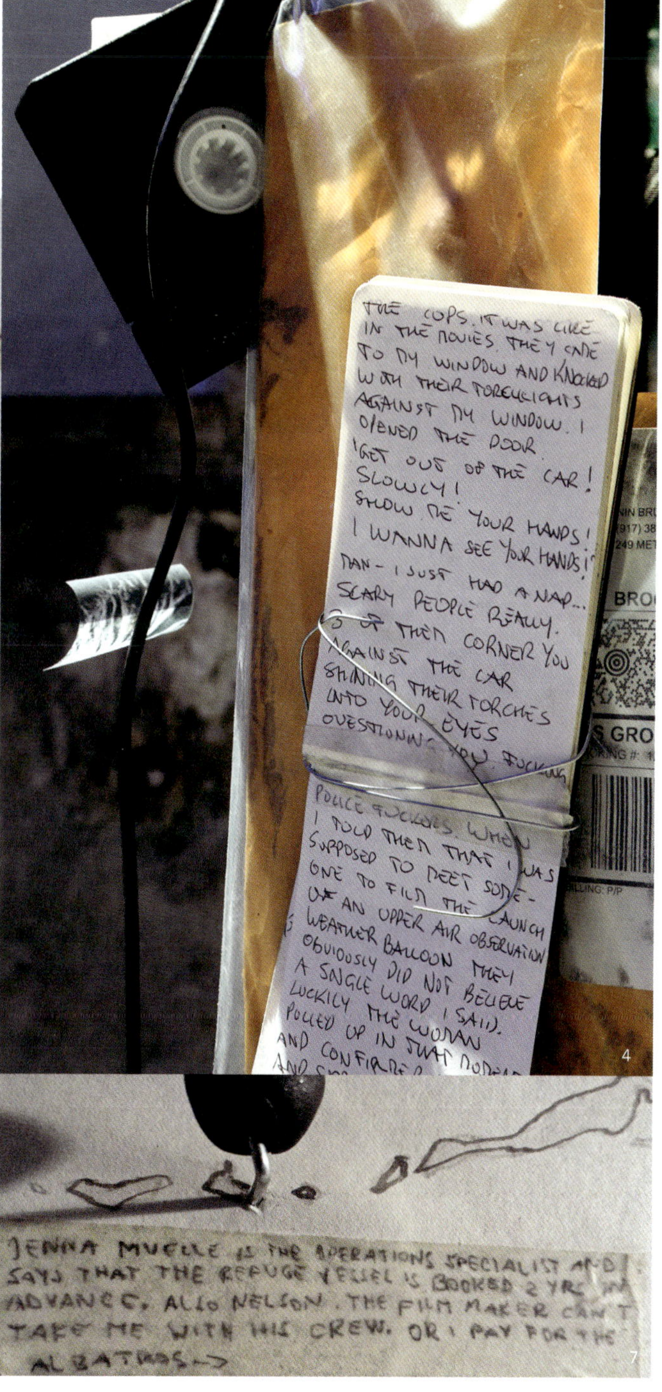

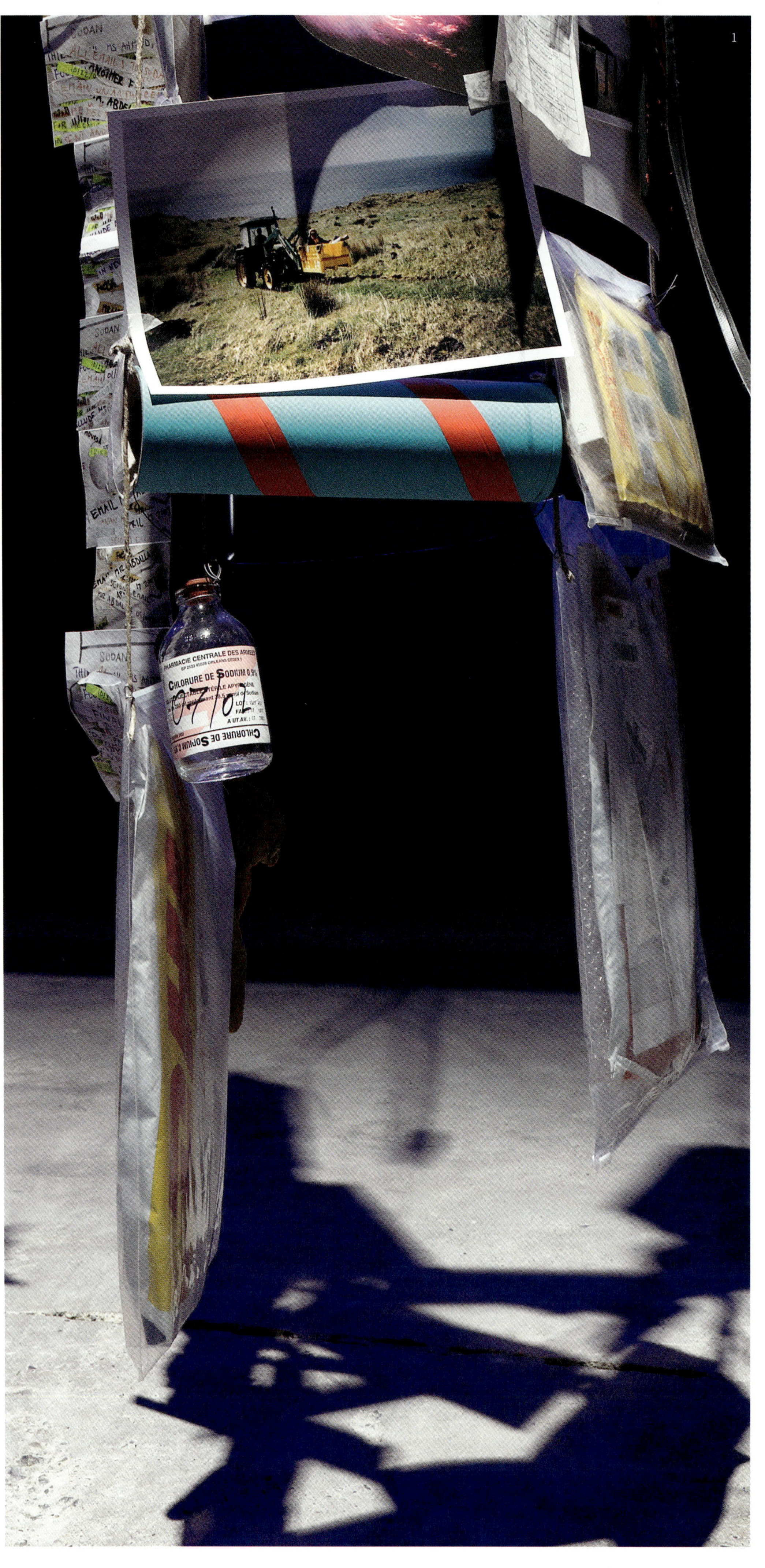

1) *Twelve O'Clock in London*, 2012, mixed media installation, dim. var., installation view Kunstraum Dornbirn (detail), photo: Robert Fessler
2) *Twelve O'Clock in London World Map*, 2010, mixed media collage on Paper, 72 x 90 x 4 inch (detail) production phase, photos: Nin Brudermann

1) On board C-130 Hercules – Performative Balloon Launch, Nin Brudermann, Jan Mayen, 2002, in collaboration with The Norwegian Meteorological Institute, The Royal Norwegian Ministry of Defense and Armed Forces, photo: crew member 2) *Twelve O'Clock in London World Map*, 2010, mixed media collage on paper, 72 x 90 x 4 inch (detail), production phase, photo: Heather Kelly 3) *Twelve O'Clock in London*, 2012, mixed media installation, dim. var., installation view Kunstraum Dornbirn (detail), photo: Robert Fessler 4) Performative Balloon Launch, Nin Brudermann, New York, 2002, photos: Hubert Dobler 5) Performative Balloon Launch, Nin Brudermann, Crozet, Indian Ocean, 2002, in collaboration with République Française Ministère de l'équipement, des transports du tourisme et de la mer – Météo-France, photo: crew member 6) *Twelve O'Clock in London*, 2010, 7 HD channel video installation TRT 22'00, video still, Performative Balloon Launch, Nin Brudermann, New York, 2002

1) *Twelve O'Clock in London: Austria/Autriche*, 2012, performance Kunstraum Dornbirn, photo: Robert Fessler 2) *Twelve O'Clock in London*, 2010, 7 HD channel video installation TRT 22'00, video still, Ministry of Environment of the Republic of Lithuania – Lithuanian Hydrometeorological Service 3) *Twelve O'Clock in London*, 2010, 7 HD channel video installation TRT 22'00, video still, Secretaría de Medio Ambiente y Recursos Naturales – Mexico Servicio Meteorologico Nacional 4) *Twelve O'Clock in London*, 2012, mixed media installation, dim. var., installation view Kunstraum Dornbirn (detail), photo: Robert Fessler 5) *Twelve O'Clock in London*, 2010, 7 HD channel video installation TRT 22'00, video still, Ministerio de Medio Ambiente de Espana – Agencia Estatal de Meteorologia 6) *Twelve O'Clock in London*, 2010, 7 HD channel video installation TRT 22'00, video still, Seychelles Ministry of the Environment and Natural Resources – National Meteorological Services

1) *Twelve O'Clock in London World Map,* 2010, mixed media collage on paper, 72 x 90 x 4 inch (detail), production phase, photo: Heather Kelly 2) *Twelve O'Clock in London,* 2010, 7 HD channel video installation TRT 22.00, video still, Empresa de Transmision Electrica S.A. de Republica de Panama – Hydrometeorology Autoridad Canal Panama Division de Ambiente 3) *Twelve O'Clock in London,* 2010, 7 HD channel video installation TRT 22'00, video stills, Performative Balloon Launch, Nin Brudermann Venice Biennale 2003, in collaboration with Makrolab and Ministero della Difesa Repubblica Italiana – Servicio Meteorologica 4) *Twelve O'Clock in London,* 2010, 7 HD channel video installation TRT 22'00, video still, Ministry of Environment, Wildlife and Tourism Department of Meteorological Services, Republic of Botswana 5) *Twelve O'Clock in London: Austria/Autriche,* 2012, performance Kunstraum Dornbirn, photo: Robert Fessler 6) On board Aurora Australis – Performative Balloon Launch, Nin Brudermann, Antarctica, 2003, in collaboration with Australian Government Commonwealth Bureau of Meteorology, photo: Greg Stone

KOREA
THINKS
OCT 5.05
DONG-CHUL SHIN
THEY ARE GOING TO
TAKE ACTION SOON
1
5

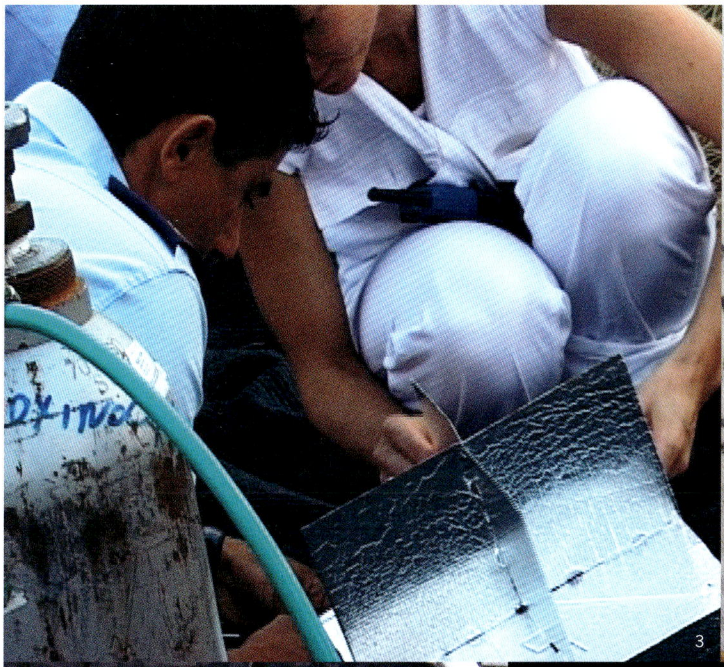

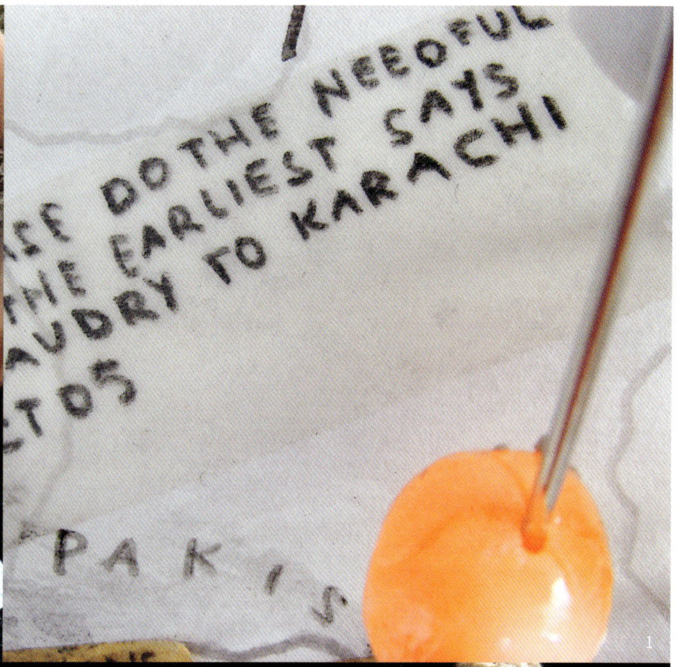

...SE DO THE NEEDFUL
THE EARLIEST SAYS
...AUDRY TO KARACHI
...T 05
PAKIS
1 
3
6
5

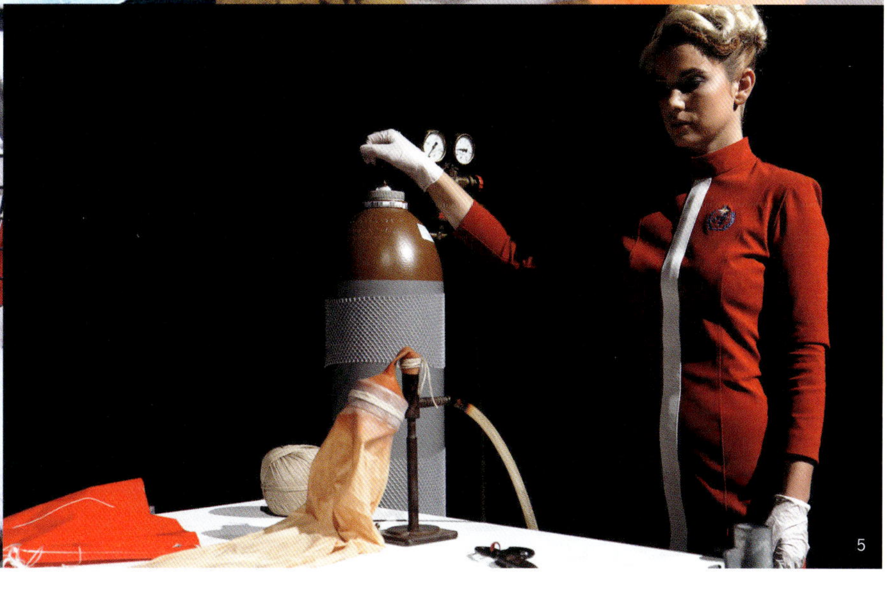

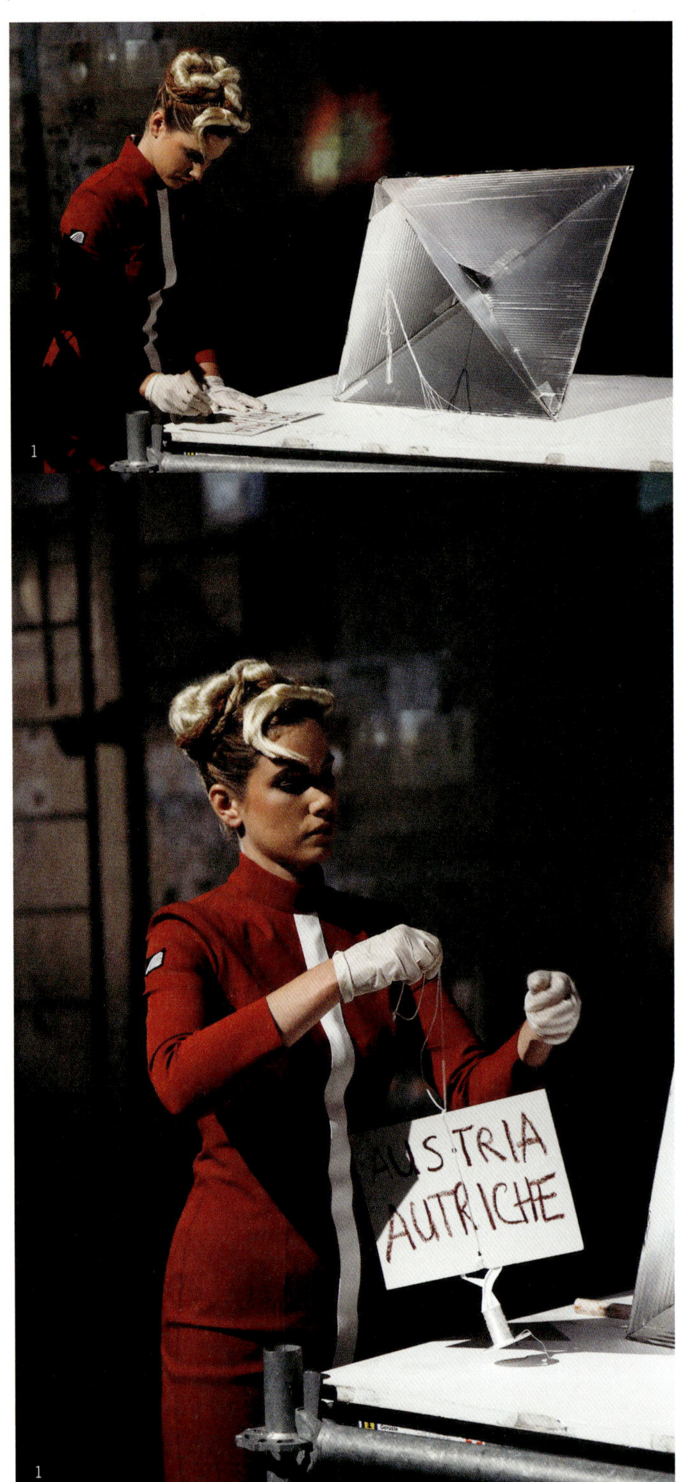

1) *Twelve O'Clock in London: Austria/Autriche,* 2012, performance Kunstraum Dornbirn, photo: Robert Fessler 2) On board Aurora Australis – Performative Balloon Launch, Nin Brudermann, Antarctica, 2003, in collaboration with Australian Government Commonwealth Bureau of Meteorology, photo: ScottS
3) *Twelve O'Clock in London,* 2010, 7 HD channel video installation TRT 22'00, video still, Performative Balloon Launch, Nin Brudermann, Venice Biennale 2003, in collaboration with Makrolab and Ministero della Difesa Repubblica Italiana – Servicio Meteorologica 4) On board Aurora Australis – Performative Balloon Launch, Nin Brudermann, Antarctica, 2003, in collaboration with Australian Government Commonwealth Bureau of Meteorology, photo: Rodney Charles
5) *Twelve O'Clock in London,* 2012, mixed media installation, dim. var., installation view Kunstraum Dornbirn (detail), photo: Robert Fessler

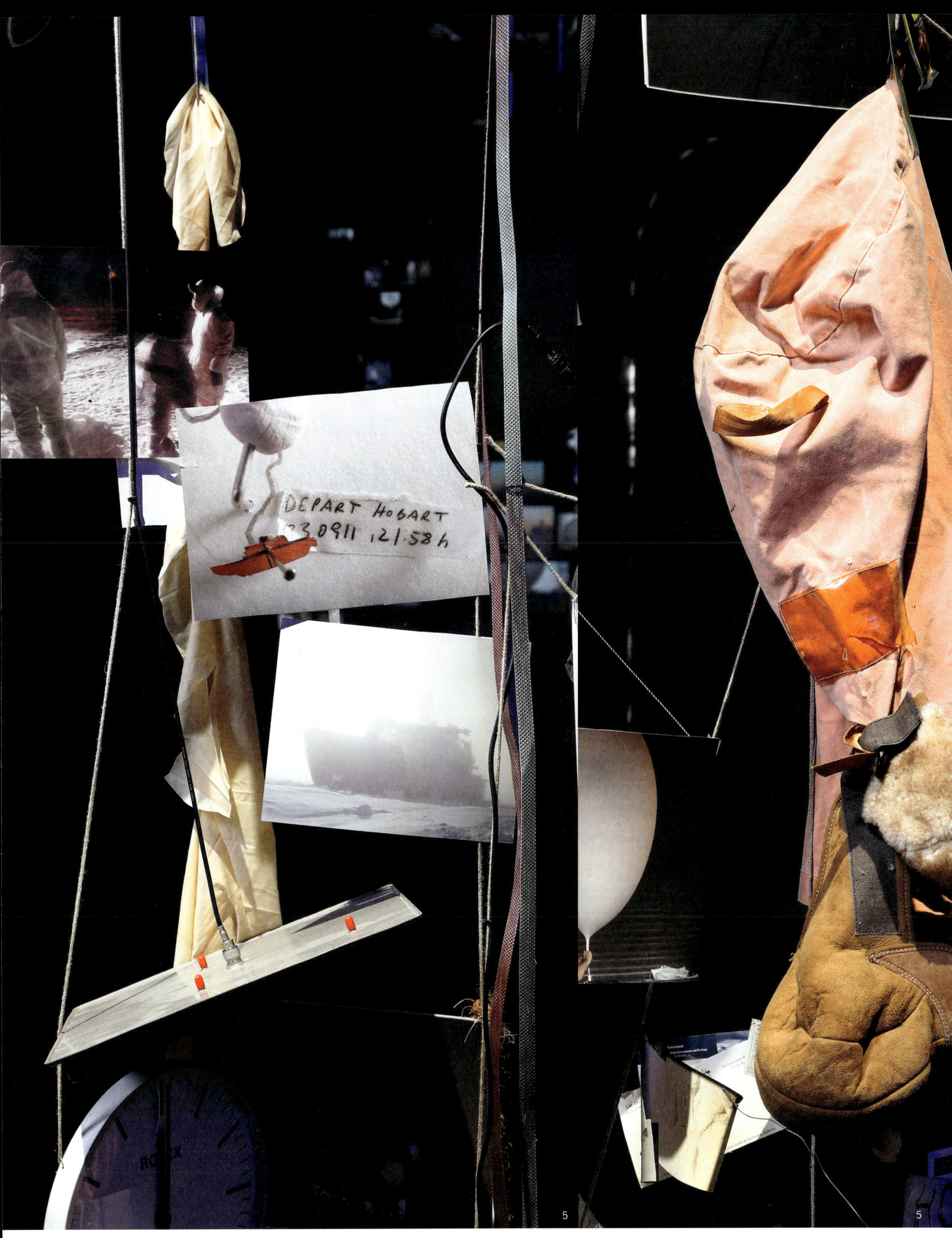
DEPART HOBART
23.09.11 12.58 h

DEPART HOBART
30911 12.55 h

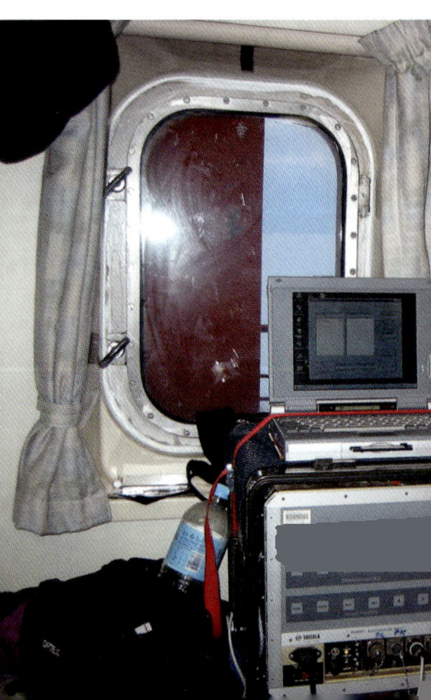

AUSTRALIS

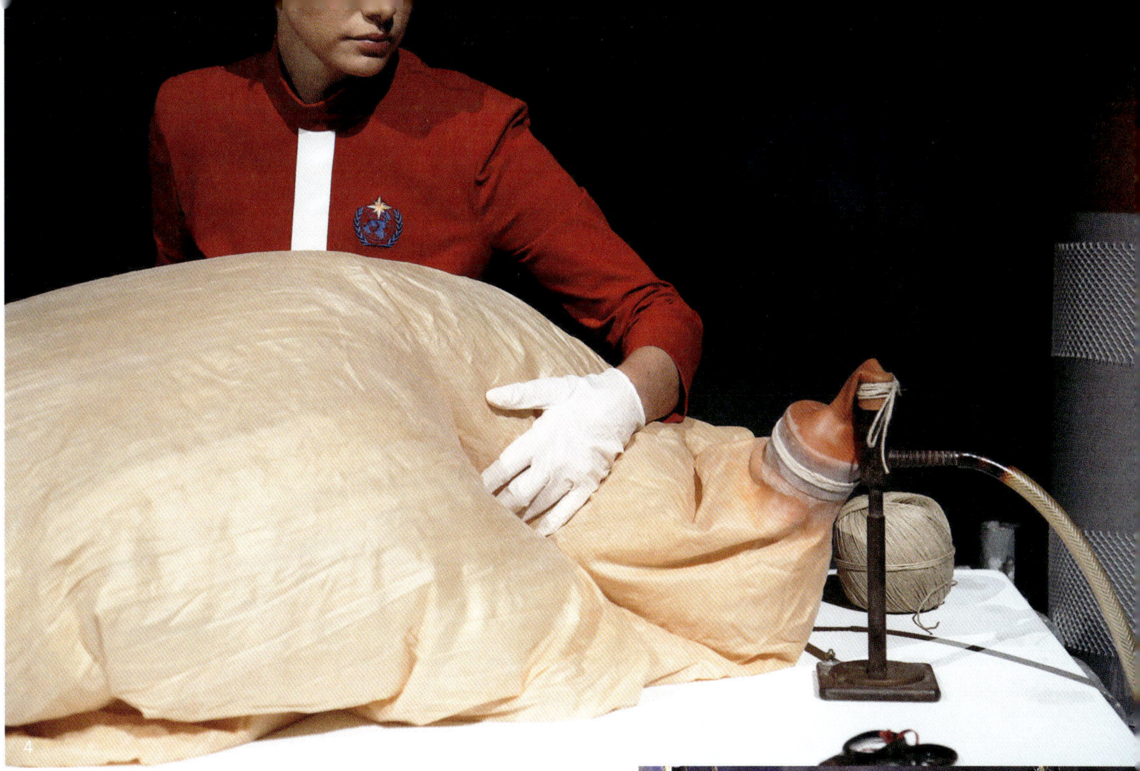

1) *Twelve O'Clock in London World Map*, 2010, mixed media collage on paper, 72 x 90 x 4 inch (detail), production phase, photo: Heather Kelly. 2) Performative Balloon Launch, Nin Brudermann, Antarctica, 2003, in collaboration with Australian Government Commonwealth Bureau of Meteorology, photo: Greg Stone
3) On board Aurora Australis – Performative Balloon Launch, Nin Brudermann, Antarctica, 2003, in collaboration with Australian Government Commonwealth Bureau of Meteorology, photo: Nin Brudermann 4) *Twelve O'Clock in London: Austria/Autriche*, 2012, performance Kunstraum Dornbirn, photo: Robert Fessler
5) *Twelve O'Clock in London*, 2012, mixed media installation, dim. var., installation view Kunstraum Dornbirn (detail), photo: Robert Fessler 6) Meteorological equipment on board Aurora Australis – Performative Balloon Launch, Nin Brudermann, Antarctica, 2003, in collaboration with Australian Government Commonwealth Bureau of Meteorology, photo: Nin Brudermann

ISRAEL
State of Israel
Ministry of Transport
Israel Meteorological Service
IMS
184 kent avenue #504
brooklyn ny 112
Brudermann
"ALLAH BE PRAISED..."
10/31/07
IT'S ON ITS WAY
FEB 7

1

2

2

1) *Twelve O'Clock in London: Austria/Autriche*, 2012, performance Kunstraum Dornbirn, photo: Robert Fessler 2) *Twelve O'Clock in London*, 2012, mixed media installation, dim. var., installation view Kunstraum Dornbirn (detail), photo: Robert Fessler 3) *Twelve O'Clock in London*, 2009, single channel video w/audio, TRT 35'00, video still, Ministry of Transport of the State of Israel – Israel Meteorological Service 4) *Twelve O'Clock in London*, 2009, single channel video w/audio, TRT 35'00, video still, Libyan National Meteorological Center – Climate and Agrometeorology Department 5) Studio shot received package Libyan National Meteorological Center – Climate and Agrometeorology Department, photo: Nin Brudermann 6) *Twelve O'Clock in London*, 2010, 7 HD channel video installation TRT 22'00, video still, Performative Balloon Launch, Nin Brudermann, Venice Biennale 2003, in collaboration with Makrolab and Ministero della Difesa Repubblica Italiana – Servicio Meteorologica

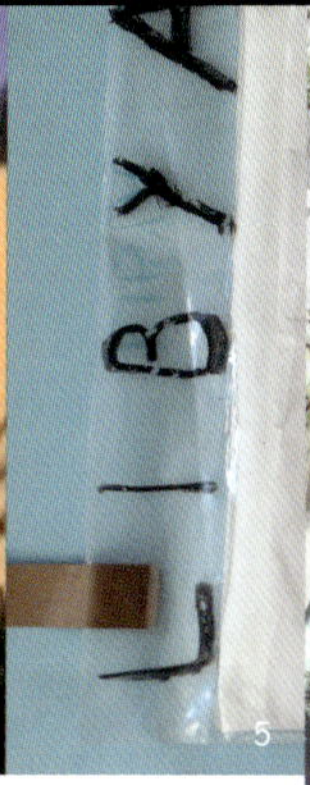

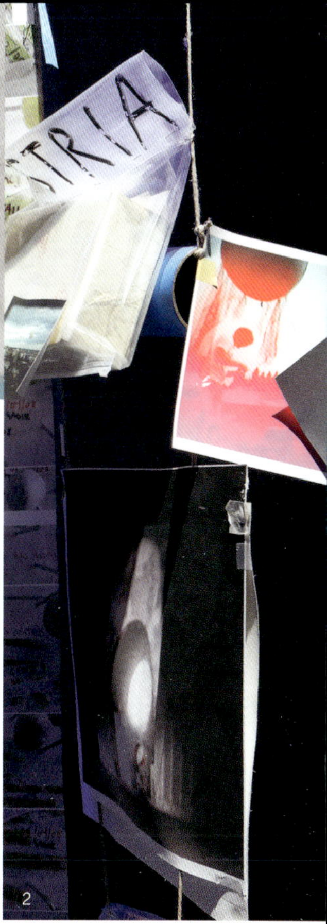

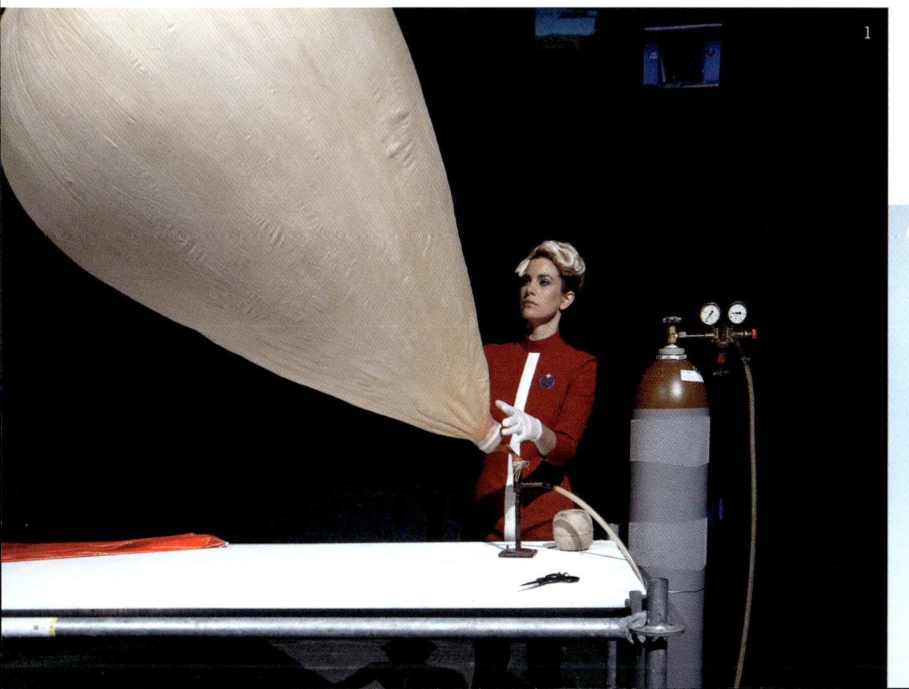

1) *Twelve O'Clock in London,* 2012, mixed media installation, dim. var., installation view Kunstraum Dornbirn (detail), photo: Robert Fessler 2) Performative Balloon Launch, Willis Island, Nin Brudermann, 2003, in collaboration with Australian Government Commonwealth Bureau of Meteorology, photo: Dave McGilvray 3) T*welve O'Clock in London,* 2010, 7 HD channel video installation TRT 22'00, video still, Performative Balloon Launch, Willis Island, Nin Brudermann, 2003, in collaboration with Australian Government Commonwealth Bureau of Meteorology 4) *Twelve O'Clock in London,* 2010, 7 HD channel video installation TRT 22'00, video still, Performative Balloon Launch, Nin Brudermann, Venice Biennale 2003, in collaboration with Makrolab and Ministero della Difesa Repubblica Italiana – Servicio Meteorologica

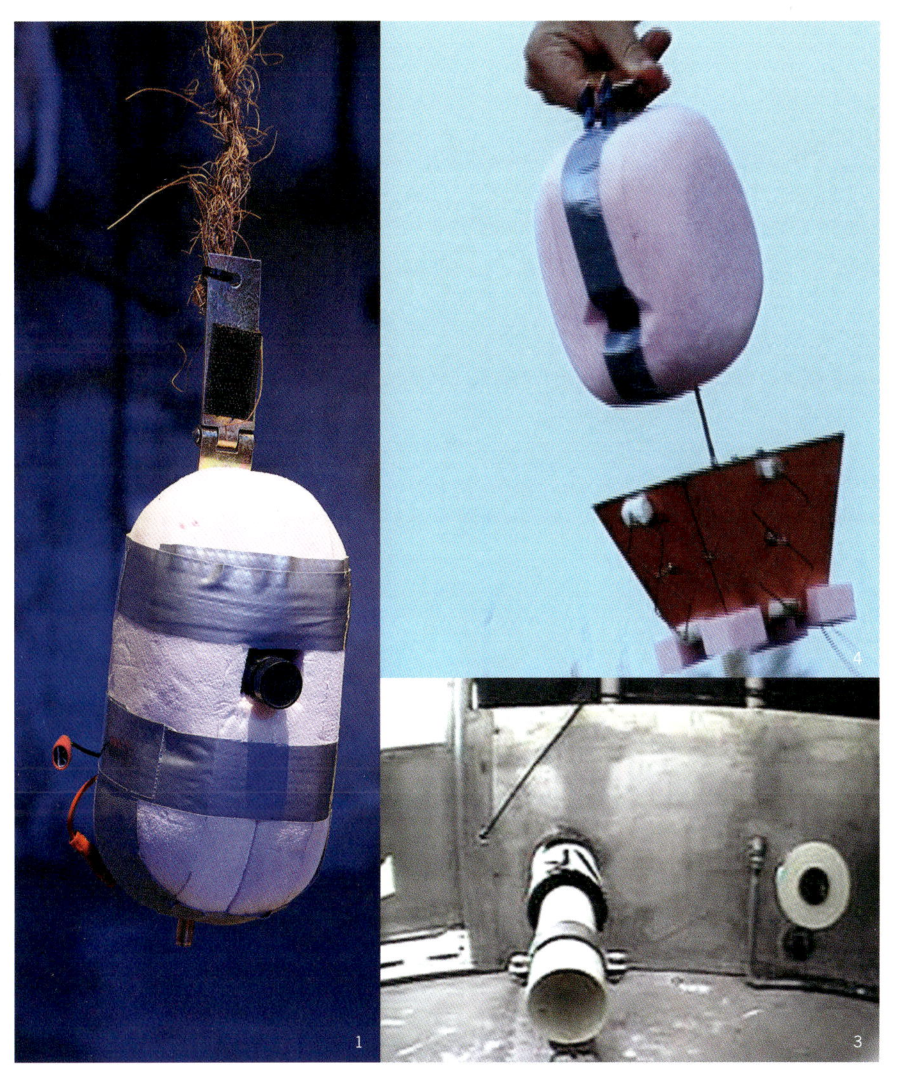

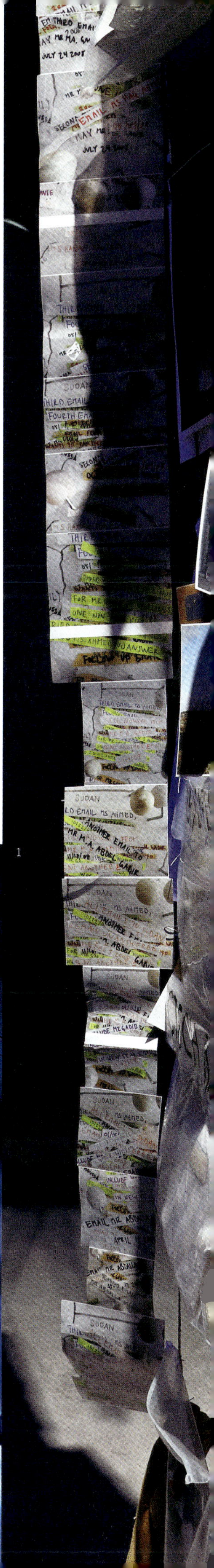

1) *Twelve O'Clock in London: Austria / Autriche,* 2012, performance Kunstraum Dornbirn, photo: Robert Fessler 2) *Twelve O'Clock in London,* 2010, 7 HD channel video installation TRT 22'00, video still, Ministry of Land Infrastructure and Transport of Japan – Japan Meteorological Agency 3) *Twelve O'Clock in London,* 2012, mixed media installation, dim. var., installation view Kunstraum Dornbirn (detail), photo: Robert Fessler 4) *Twelve O'Clock in London,* 2010, 7 HD channel video installation TRT 22'00, video still, United States Department of Commerce – U.S. National Oceanic & Atmospheric Administration

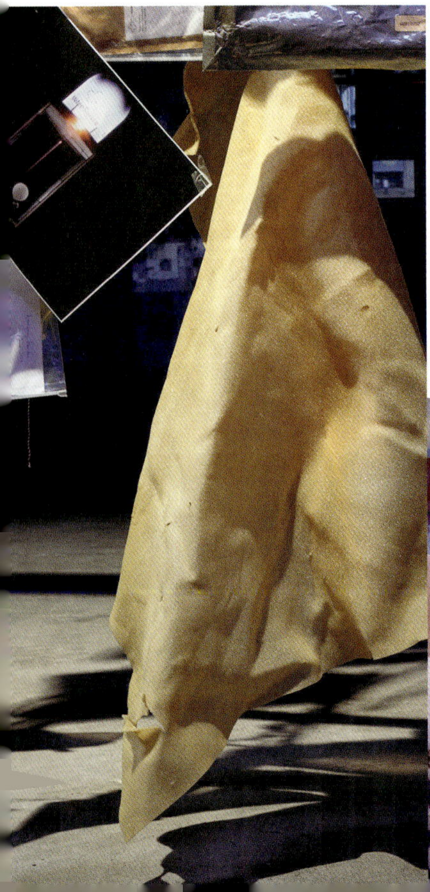

Twelve O'Clock in London, 2012, mixed media installation, dim. var.,
installation view Kunstraum Dornbirn (details), photos: Robert Fessler

NO BALLOONS OR GAS IN MALAWI
CANNOT RE-SHOOT
THIRD
MUCHINDA
BANGLADESH
PAKISTAN
ARGENTINA
Bertha Kély
Production Assistance
Twelve O'Clock in London
249 Metropolitan Avenue 2nd Floor
Brooklyn NY 11211
USA

Dieter Buchhart

Der Regelbruch des Homo ludens

Spätestens seit Marcel Duchamp haben sich zahlreiche KünstlerInnen mit Spielen, Spielmechanismen, Spielästhetik und Spielstrategien beschäftigt. KünstlerInnen wie Yoko Ono und Öyvind Fahlström erweiterten, basierend auf Marcel Duchamps Ready-mades und John Cages Einführung des Zufalls, mit ihrer Beschäftigung mit Partizipation, Spielen und Spielregeln den Kunstbegriff hin zum „experimentellen" Spiel. Den BetrachterInnen wird eine entscheidende Rolle nicht nur als RezipientInnen, sondern auch als aktive PartizipantInnen zugewiesen und eine handlungsbestimmte Funktion für die BesucherInnen als AkteurInnen geschaffen.

Seit der Mitte der 1990er Jahre lässt sich, angetrieben von der Hochkonjunktur der elektronischen Spiele, eine verstärkte Auseinandersetzung mit Spielen in der zeitgenössischen Kunst feststellen. Diese ist nicht auf bestimmte Medien beschränkt, sondern findet sich in Grafiken, Gemälden, installativen und performativen Werken bis hin zu Radio-, TV-, Computer- oder Internetarbeiten in unterschiedlichsten Ausprägungen. Zahlreiche KünstlerInnen adaptieren gängige Spiele, setzen dabei auf Wiedererkennungseffekte und versuchen, die Angebote unserer Spaßgesellschaft zu transformieren, zu konterkarieren und aktuelle gesellschaftspolitische Fragen aufzuwerfen. So wurden in den letzten Jahren von KünstlerInnen eine Reihe von Brettspielen, unzählige Computer- und Internetspiele bis hin zu psychologischen Spielen produziert, die den Handlungsrahmen[1] der SpielerInnen recht unterschiedlich festlegen, häufig jedoch den Handlungsspielraum der AkteurInnen mit den Spielregeln und den festgelegten Grundparametern des Spiels sehr eng setzen und die Öffnung des Kunstbegriffes in Hinblick auf Interaktion mit einem geschlossenen Handlungsfeld erkaufen. Selten wird das Korsett der Regeln gesprengt, vielmehr die Kunst diesen untergeordnet.

Nin Brudermann nutzt Spielmechanismen, Spielästhetik und Spielstrategien in unterschiedlicher Weise in ihren Kunstprojekten, welche die immerwährende Dualität von Wirklichkeit und Fiktion aufzeigen. Stets steht eine umfassende Recherche zu Beginn eines jeden ihrer umfangreichen Projekte. Auf die Themen und Geschichten stößt die Künstlerin dabei durch Zufall, eine der Grundlagen des Spiels. So entwickelte sich die Installation *Aurelio Z* aus einem Fundstück, einer kleinen Kommode, welche die Künstlerin als Badezimmermöbel verwendete. Darin entdeckte sie eine Reihe von Gegenstän-

Dieter Buchhart

Homo Ludens Breaks the Rules

No later than Marcel Duchamp's amuse-art, artists have become engrossed in the playful, i.e., in the mechanisms, the aesthetics and the strategies of play. Inspired by Duchamp's ready-mades and John Cage's introduction of chance, artists like Yoko Ono and Övyind Fahlström – in their engagement with participation, play and its rules – have expanded the definition of art to include the "experimental" game. Viewers are assigned a crucial role, not only as recipients but also as active participants, and visitors as co-players are given a decision-making function.

Since the mid-1990s and propelled by the boom in electronic games, contemporary art has increasingly taken up play as a subject. This is not limited to specific media, but is found in graphic art, paintings, installative and performative works, all the way to those in radio, TV, computer or Internet in greatly diverse manifestations. Many artists adapt stock games, rely on the aha effect of recognition and seek to transform and counteract our society's fun-loving overtures, while raising current social and political questions. Thus, over the past years, artists have produced a series of board games, countless computer and Internet games, up to psychological games that establish the players' framework of action[1] in quite different ways. Often enough the wiggle room the rules and the fixed parameters of the game allowed the actors is very narrow, and the opening up of the definition of art as regards interaction is then confronted with a confined field of activity. The restraining corset of rules is seldom broken, rather it is art that is made subordinate to them.

Nin Brudermann, in various ways, deploys the mechanisms, the aesthetics and the strategies of play in her art projects, which underline the constant duality between reality and fiction. Intense research stands at the beginning of each one of her comprehensive projects. The artist hereby arrives at her themes and stories per chance, which is one of the ground rules of play. For instance, the installation *Aurelio Z* was developed from a found object, a small commode that the artist used as bathroom furniture. In it she discovered a series of articles, among other things, a membership card of Aurelio Z. to a video rental store or a letter to the Secret Service. After very intensive research, Brudermann managed to link all these objects and their inbuilt stories with each other, along with incidents in World War II and

den unter anderem auch eine Mitgliedskarte einer Videothek eines Aurelio Z. oder einen Brief an den Secret Service. Nach einer eingehenden Recherche gelang es Brudermann, all diese Gegenstände und die Geschichten, die diese in sich tragen, miteinander und mit Ereignissen des Zweiten Weltkrieges bis hin zum Superdollar, einem hochwertig gefälschten 100-Dollarschein[2], und zeitgeschichtlichen Ereignissen zu verbinden. Es gelang ihr, ein atemberaubend spannendes Projekt zu entwickeln, welches sie in der 2008 performten Version in der Kunsthalle Krems zu einer Gameshow umgestaltet hatte. Zwei ausgewählte Spieler mussten zum Fall des Aurelio Z. Fragen der Moderatorin, eines New Yorker Models, beantworten. Die BesucherInnen wurden als MitspielerInnen zur Partizipation verpflichtet, um den Spielern im Falle

Aurelio Z: The Game, Nin Brudermann, 2008,
mixed media installation / performance,
performance view *Go NYC*, Kunsthalle Krems, 2008

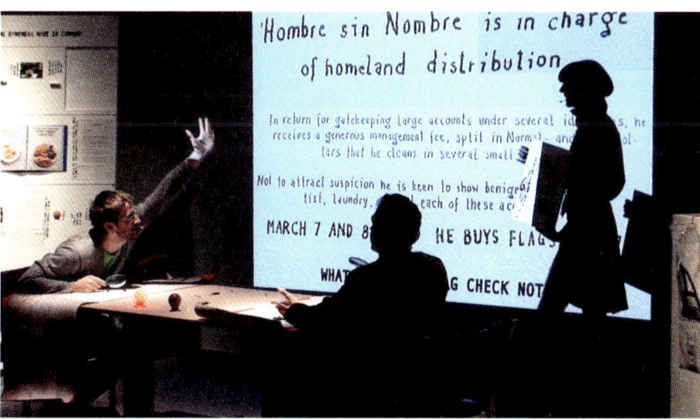

einer falschen Antwort auszuhelfen. Für jede richtige Antwort erhielten diese jeweils einen Superdollar. Dabei betreibt Brudermann ein sehr glaubhaftes Vexierspiel von Wissenschaftsrealtainment, Relikten aus der Wissenschaft als (scheinbare) Beweisstücke des Echten und aus dem Genre des Films und des Geschichtenerzählens. Mit ihrer Gameshow reflektiert sie nicht nur den alltäglich im Fernsehen inszenierten Kampf um das Geld diverser Game- und Quizshows zur Erzielung einer möglichst hohen Einschaltquote, sondern stellt den Homo ludens, den Menschen als Spieler, in den Mittelpunkt des Werkes. Ganz im Sinne von Vilém Flusser, der die Meinung vertrat, dass das Spiel als Gesellschaftsspiel die Möglichkeit biete, das scheinbar Nichtzusammengehörige, das Inkohärente im Netz zusammenzufügen, wo sich Wahrheit allein im Spiel in immer neuen Zuordnungen bilde, im Suchen freier Valenzen, im Lösen, Verlieren und jähen Wiederfinden.[3] Stets in dem Verständnis, dass das Zusammen- und Ineinandergreifen von Zufall und Regel als Modell des Spiels unserer Kultur zugrunde liege. Die Dominanz des Homo ludens, der heute alle Bereiche des Lebens und des Alltags erobert hat, wie das Realtainment von „Big Brother", Sportberichterstattung mit Helmkameras, die Überschüttung mit Rätsel- und Gewinnspielen oder interaktives Fernsehen, Internetspiele und Avatare belegen, enttarnt die Künstlerin in ihren Gesellschaftsspielen eindrucksvoll. Dabei verbindet

up to the so-called superdollar,[2] a high quality counterfeit 100 dollar bill, and to current events. She succeeded in developing all these into a breathtakingly exciting project that she then, in the 2008 performed version, reworked into a game show for Kunsthalle Krems. Two selected players had to provide answers to questions the moderator asked about the case of Aurelio Z. Visitors as co-players were recruited to participate and help out when a wrong answer was given. For every right answer, each player was given one superdollar. Whereby Brudermann played a credible flip-flop game of scientific realtainment, with scientific relics as (seeming) evidence of authenticity, in contrast to those of the film genre and of storytelling. With her game show, she reflected not only the everyday TV-staged contest to win money on diverse game and quiz shows as an attempt to attain the channel's highest possible audience ratings, but set homo ludens – man as player – at the center of the work. Quite in the sense of Vilém Flusser, who was of the opinion that play as society's game offers the possibility for the seemingly uncorrelated and incoherent to come together in the Net, where truth is meant to form itself into ever new relationships solely through play, in our search for free valences, in unloosing, losing and sudden rediscovering.[3] And always with the understanding that the concurrence and interlocking of

chance with the order of rules lies at the foundation of our culture as a game model. In her play on society, the artist impressively unmasks the dominance of homo ludens, or playful man, who has conquered all areas of life and the everyday world, as evidenced by the reality show "Big Brother", sport reportage with helmet cameras, the deluge of puzzle-solving and competitive games or interactive television, Internet games and avatars. She hereby links homo ludens with a society built on its faith in science and at the same time opens our eyes to the absurdity of our lack of critique of science and of its many specialized scientific activities. She not only calls human existence per se into question, but also what we in our entertainment society assume to be reality.

In 2004 in her work with the *NASD Projekt Fledermaus* (Bat Project) she infiltrated the parallel world of the (natural) sciences. In the U.S. Navy's former military zone on Puerto Rico's Vieques Island, she – in collaboration with bat specialists – studied the daily routine of the new winged inhabitants who had settled in the former munitions depot after the humans deserted the now ghostly bunker landscape. It was similar to the *Twelve O'Clock in London* project, for which her intense engagement with the phenomenon of weather balloons constituted the basis. With it she created a world-encompassing art project based on the idea that every day at 12 o'clock Lon-

sie den Homo ludens mit unserer auf Wissenschafts-gläubigkeit aufgebauten Gesellschaft und führt zu-gleich die Absurdität der fehlenden Wissenschafts-kritik und manch spezialisierter wissenschaftlicher Aktivitäten vor Augen. So hinterfragt sie nicht nur das menschliche Sein an sich, sondern auch das, was wir in unserer Unterhaltungsgesellschaft als Realität vermuten.

2004 drang sie bereits in ihrer Arbeit mit dem *NASD Projekt Fledermaus* in die Parallelwelt der (Na-tur-)Wissenschaften ein. Sie untersuchte auf dem ehemals militärischen Gebiet der U.S. Navy der pu-ertoricanischen Insel Vieques gemeinsam mit Fleder-mausspezialisten, die tagein tagaus in den ehemali-gen Munitionsdepots derselben Routine nachgehen, die neuen Bewohner dieser von Menschen verlasse-

nen geisterhaften Bunkerlandschaft. Ebenso in dem Projekt *Twelve O'Clock in London*, in dem ihre inten-sive Auseinandersetzung mit dem Phänomen der Wetterballone die Grundlage bildet. Dabei schuf sie ein weltumspannendes Kunstprojekt, basierend auf der Idee, dass man jeden Tag um zwölf Uhr Londo-ner Zeit in sämtlichen Ländern und Regionen unserer Welt gleichzeitig die Wetterballone zur Abklärung der Wettersituation steigen lässt. Die Ballone schweben in den Himmel, blähen sich mit zunehmender Dis-tanz zur Erde auf, bis sie schlussendlich zerplatzen. Brudermann stattete ihre Ballone, die sie bei den verschiedensten Wetterstationen weltweit unter an-derem auch in der Antarktis steigen ließ, nicht nur mit einer Kamera aus, sondern forderte weltweit Wetterstationen in Australien, im Iran, in Pakistan,

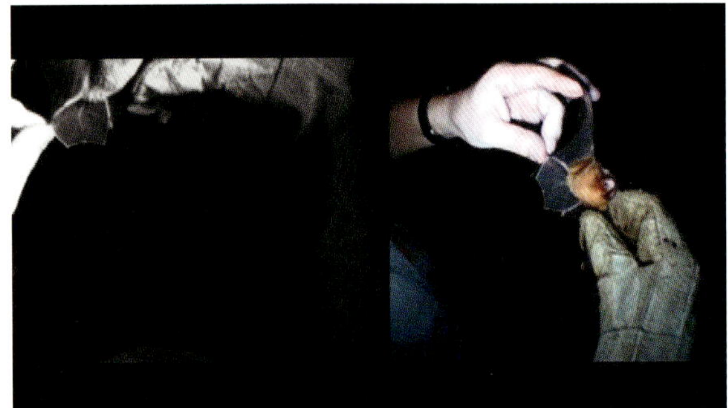

NASD Projekt Fledermaus,
Nin Brudermann, 2004, 2 channel video,
sound (37 min), video still

Twelve O'Clock in London World Map, Nin Brudermann, 2010,
mixed media collage on paper, 72 x 90 x 4 inch (detail),
exhibition view Kunstraum Dornbirn, photo: Robert Fessler

don time, weather balloons are simultaneously un-loosed into the air in all the countries and regions of the world so as to clarify the weather situation. The balloons float in the sky, continue to inflate with in-creasing distance to the earth, until they finally burst. Brudermann sent balloons up worldwide from the most diverse weather stations, also from the Antarctic among others. She not only equipped them with a camera, but has also championed a global coverage of weather stations from Australia, Iran, Pakistan, China, the U.S. or Chile, prompting each country to produce its own balloon videos and send them on to her. Her, literally, people-connecting pro-ject not only transcends national borders, but invites a large number of players to participate. The game board is a hand-drawn map on which all the players, plus those who can still be recruited, are recorded. She then brings the countless videos together in a large-scale projection made up of the innumerable individual shots from the perspective of the balloons, which slowly increase in size and, in the end, are shown as they burst. Game over for the individual counter. May the next game begin. The weather bal-loon is here a counter on a global game board that brings together what is supposedly incompatible and antagonistic: that which seems feasible only outside the ordinary and the conceivable. Play as a game of chance and as a utopia.

Brudermann in *Twelve O'Clock in London* breaks the rules of our world's friend-foe schema by outlin-ing a way of overcoming the insurmountable. In con-trast, in the *Late Night Show*, she allows little hope of a "better" world. She skillfully pulls out all the stops that realtainment deploys to produce a board game in Flusser's sense: in her 2010 performance at the Copenhagen ME Gallery, a moderator intro-duced a woman who presented a series of articles to the audience at a Saturday night show. What be-gan as seemingly harmless and effortless entertain-ment evolved into an ice-cold psycho thriller. Name-ly during the performance, the woman revealed herself to be a pathological stalker. The initial smiles of the unprepared moderator and the audience froze when the dramatic details of her craze became ap-parent. The expected easily consumable entertain-ment of an evening show turned into the brutal re-porting of a fight for survival. The entertainer became both perpetrator and victim, who held the mirror up to the voyeuristic spectators of our media-hungry society, now in shock because the confined space allowed no escape. That which seemed unre-lated, came together in unloosing, losing and the sudden rediscovering of new constellations and ex-periences. Brudermann defines a new space for act-ing and experiencing without the comfort of the abil-ity to flee "real" life.

China, den USA oder Chile auf, ihr jeweils eigenes Ballonvideo anzufertigen und an sie zu senden. Ihr buchstäblich völkerverbindendes Projekt überschreitet nicht nur die Landesgrenzen, sondern lädt eine große Anzahl von SpielerInnen ein zu partizipieren. Das Spielbrett ist dabei eine handgezeichnete Karte, in der alle MitspielerInnen und jene, die noch welche werden können, verzeichnet sind. Die vielen Videos führt sie in einer großflächigen Projektion aus zahlreichen individuellen Aufnahmen aus Perspektive der Ballons zusammen, die langsam an Größe zunehmen und schlussendlich platzen. Game over für die individuelle Spielfigur. Das nächste Spiel mag beginnen. Der Wetterballon als Spielfigur am globalen Spielbrett, die scheinbar Nichtzusammengehöriges, Verfeindetes für einen Augenblick verbindet. Was nur im Außerhalb des Gewöhnlichen und Denkbaren machbar scheint. Das Spiel als Chance und als Utopie.

Während Brudermann in *Twelve O'Clock in London* die Regeln des Freund-Feind-Schemas unserer Welt bricht, eine Möglichkeit der Überwindung des Unüberwindbaren andeutet, verbleibt in *Late Night Show* nur wenig Hoffnung auf eine „bessere" Welt. Souverän spielt sie auf der Klaviatur des Realtainments als Gesellschaftsspiel im Flusser'schem Sinn: In ihrer Performance 2010 in der Kopenhagener Galerie ME stellte ein Moderator eine Frau vor, die dem Publikum der Samstagnachtshow eine Reihe von

Gegenständen präsentierte. Was scheinbar harmlos als leichtgängige Unterhaltung begann, entwickelte sich zum eiskalten Psychothriller. Denn im Zuge der Performance deklarierte sich die Frau als eine krankhafte Stalkerin. Das anfängliche Lächeln des unvorbereiteten Moderators und des Publikums gefror, als die dramatischen Details dieses Wahns offensichtlich wurden. Die zu erwartende leicht konsumierbare Unterhaltung einer Nachtshow geriet zur brutalen Schilderung eines Überlebenskampfes. Die Unterhalterin wurde zur Täterin und zum Opfer, die den zum Voyeurismus angehaltenen Anwesenden unserer mediengeilen Gesellschaft im Schock den Spiegel vorhielten, da es durch die räumliche Nähe kein Entrinnen gab. Scheinbar Nichtzusammengehöriges fügte sich im Lösen, Verlieren und

Late Night Show, Nin Brudermann, 2010, HD DVD video w/sound 43 min, performance view, ME Contemporary, Copenhagen 2010

In her projects, Brudermann adapts a game's usual strategies, aesthetics, and mechanisms and depends on the aha effect of recognition, on the one hand, so as to lull the audience into a sense of security, not only to transform what our fun-loving society has on offer, but to break with it. Games, normally "perceived as being outside of normal life",[4] offer Brudermann the possibility to raise many current social, political and aesthetic questions. She breaks the restraining corset of rules and, along with participating actors and the audience, skillfully lays bare an open field of action, often within a tense psycho-social situation. Using and abusing game strategies, she succeeds in getting the actors to participate with a high degree of freedom, while simultaneously making them aware of their very lack of room for maneuver, of their unfreedom. Opening up art to play entails opening up a concept of art based on the participation of the recipients, a concept that is negotiated against the backdrop to a dialectic of form and openness, game rules, and a certain measure of freedom. The degree of the participants' freedom is established, on the one hand, by the artist and, on the other, by the courageousness of the actors to breach the rules. Brudermann fights for the freedom and the courage to recognize and experience something new before the game even ends.

[1] Johan Huizinga: *Homo Ludens*, 1938.

[2] "A superdollar (also known as a superbill or supernote) is a very high quality counterfeit United States one hundred-dollar bill. In 2011 government sources state that these 'counterfeit bills were in worldwide circulation from the late 1980s until at least July 2000 …' Various groups have been suspected. […] The U.S. government believes that these notes were most likely produced in North Korea." Cited from en.wikipedia.org/wiki/Superdollar. Reference date: 29 June 2010.

[3] Vilém Flusser: "Gesellschaftsspiele" in: *Kunstforum International,* Vol. 116, Ruppichteroth, November-December 1991, p. 66ff. On Flusser see among others, Vilém Flusser: *Ins Universum der technischen Bilder*, Göttingen 1989; Vilém Flusser: "Gesellschaftsspiele" in: Georg Hartwagner, Stefan Iglhaut, Florian Rötzer (ed.): *Künstliche Spiele*, Munich 1993.

[4] Johan Huizinga: *Homo Ludens*, 1938.

jähen Wiederfinden zu neuen Konstellationen und Erfahrungen zusammen. Brudermann definierte einen neuen Handlungs- und Erfahrungsraum, ohne dem Wohlgefühl, dem „eigentlichen" Leben zu entfliehen. In ihren Projekten adaptiert Brudermann gängige Spielstrategien, Spielästhetik und Spielmechanismen und setzt dabei einerseits auf Wiedererkennungseffekte, um das Publikum in Sicherheit zu wiegen, um dann die Angebote unserer Spaßgesellschaft nicht nur zu transformieren, sondern mit diesen zu brechen. Da Spiele zumeist als „außerhalb des gewöhnlichen Lebens stehend empfunden werden",[4] bieten sie Brudermann die Möglichkeit, zahlreiche aktuelle gesellschaftliche, politische und ästhetische Fragen aufzuwerfen. Sie sprengt das Korsett der Regeln, öffnet souverän mithilfe der Partizipation von AkteurInnen und Publikum ein offenes Handlungsfeld, häufig im psychosozialen Spannungsraum. Es gelingt ihr mittels der Benutzung und Ausnutzung von Spielstrategien, die AkteurInnen zur Partizipation mit hohem Freiheitsgrad zu bewegen und ihnen zugleich den mangelnden Spielraum, ihre Unfreiheit, vor Augen zu führen. Die Öffnung der Kunst für das Spiel bedeutet eine auf der Partizipation der RezipientInnen basierende Öffnung des Kunstbegriffs, die jedoch stets vor der Dialektik von Form und Offenheit, Spielregeln und Freiheitsgrad verhandelt wird. Der Freiheitsgrad der PartizipantInnen wird einerseits von der Künstlerin und andererseits vom Mut der AkteurInnen zum Regelverstoß festgelegt. Brudermann kämpft für die Freiheit und den Mut, noch vor Spielende Neues zu erkennen und zu erfahren.

[1] Johan Huizinga: *Homo Ludens. Vom Ursprung der Kultur im Spiel*, Reinbek bei Hamburg 2001 (Originalausgabe 1938), S. 22.

[2] „Der Begriff Superdollar (oder auch Supernote) wurde geprägt, als US-amerikanische Geheimdienste etwa 1994 auf gefälschte Banknoten von einer derartigen Güte stießen, dass sie kaum mehr vom Original zu unterscheiden waren. Dabei handelt es sich um 100-US-Dollar-Banknoten, die auf sehr hochwertigem Papier mit hoher Druckqualität hergestellt wurden. Nach umfangreichen Ermittlungen wird angenommen, dass sie aus dem Office 39 der nordkoreanischen Regierung stammen." Zitiert nach http://de.wikipedia.org/wiki/Superdollar, Stichtag 27. 3. 2012.

[3] Vilém Flusser: „Gesellschaftsspiele". In: *Kunstforum international*, Bd. 116, Ruppichteroth November–Dezember 1991, S. 66ff. Zu Flusser vgl. u.a. Vilém Flusser: *Ins Universum der technischen Bilder*, Göttingen 1989; Vilém Flusser: „Gesellschaftsspiele". In: Georg Hartwagner, Stefan Iglhaut, Florian Rötzer (Hg.): *Künstliche Spiele*, München 1993.

[4] Johan Huizinga: *Homo Ludens. Vom Ursprung der Kultur im Spiel*, Reinbek bei Hamburg 2001 (Originalausgabe 1938), S. 22.

Twelve O'Clock in London: Austria/Autriche, 2012, mixed media installation view Kunstraum Dornbirn, photo: Robert Fessler

1) *Twelve O'Clock in London: Austria/Autriche,* 2012, performance Kunstraum Dornbirn, photo: Robert Fessler 2) Studio shot received package Pakistan Ministry of Defense – Pakistan Meteorological Department, photo: Nin Brudermann 3) *Twelve O'Clock in London,* 2010, 7 HD channel video installation TRT 22'00, video still, Pakistan Ministry of Defense – Pakistan Meteorological Department 4) *Twelve O'Clock in London,* 2010, 7 HD channel video installation TRT 22'00, video still, State Council of the People's Republic of China – China Meteorological Administration 5) *Twelve O'Clock in London World Map,* 2010, mixed media collage on paper, 72 x 90 x 4 inch (detail), production phase, photo: Heather Kelly 6) *Twelve O'Clock in London,* 2010, 7 HD channel video installation TRT 22'00, video still, LR Ministry of Environment of the Republic of Latvia – Latvian Environment Geology and Meteorology Agency 7) *Twelve O'Clock in London World Map,* 2010, mixed media collage on Paper, 72 x 90 x 4 inch (detail), exhibition view Kunstraum Dornbirn, photo: Robert Fessler

ON PAKISTAN STATE SERVICE

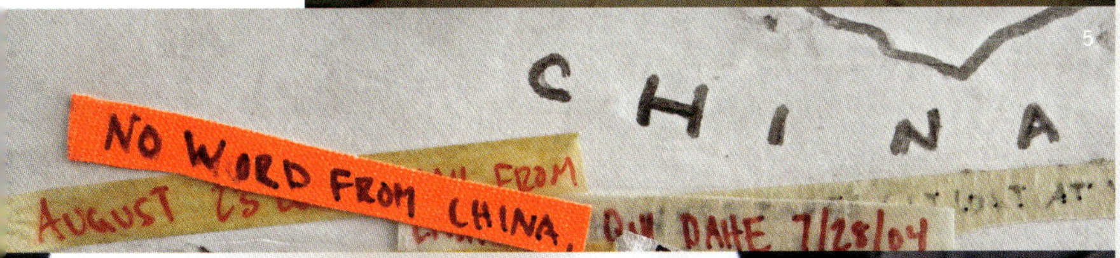

CHINA
NO WORD FROM CHINA
AUGUST
ON DATE 7/28/04

GOT
THE
TAPES

Twelve O'Clock in London: Austria/Autriche, 2012, performance Kunstraum Dornbirn, photo: Robert Fessler

Twelve O'Clock In London: Austria/Autriche
Nin Brudermann 2012

HD video / sound
Produced by Kunstraum Dornbirn, 2012,
as live performance at the opening reception of
Nin Brudermann – Twelve O'Clock in London: Austria/Autriche

Christine Bock as Austrian Meteorological Representative
Meteorological Assistant: Arnold Tschofen, ZAMG Austria
Door Openers: Adrian Wehinger and Felix Hagen
Camera: Hansjoerg Kapeller, Konstantin Ammann
Set Design: Nin Brudermann
Stage Lighting: Alex Schwendinger
Technical Installation: Martin Beck
Costume: Elisabeth Nachbaur
Hair Styling and Make-Up: Katrin Burtscher

With great thanks to: Christina Nägele – Regionale XII,
Michael Staudinger and Mag. Roland Potzmann – Zentralanstalt für Meteorolgie
und Geodynamik Österreich, Petra Dobler, Marianne Musek and Stefanie Lingg,
Anna Karina Hofbauer, Hans Dünser and the team of Kunstraum Dornbirn.

1) *Twelve O'Clock in London: Austria/Autriche,* 2012, performance Kunstraum Dornbirn,
photo: Robert Fessler 2) *Twelve O'Clock in London,* 2010, 7 HD channel video installation TRT
22'00, exhibition view Kunstraum Dornbirn (details), photos: Robert Fessler

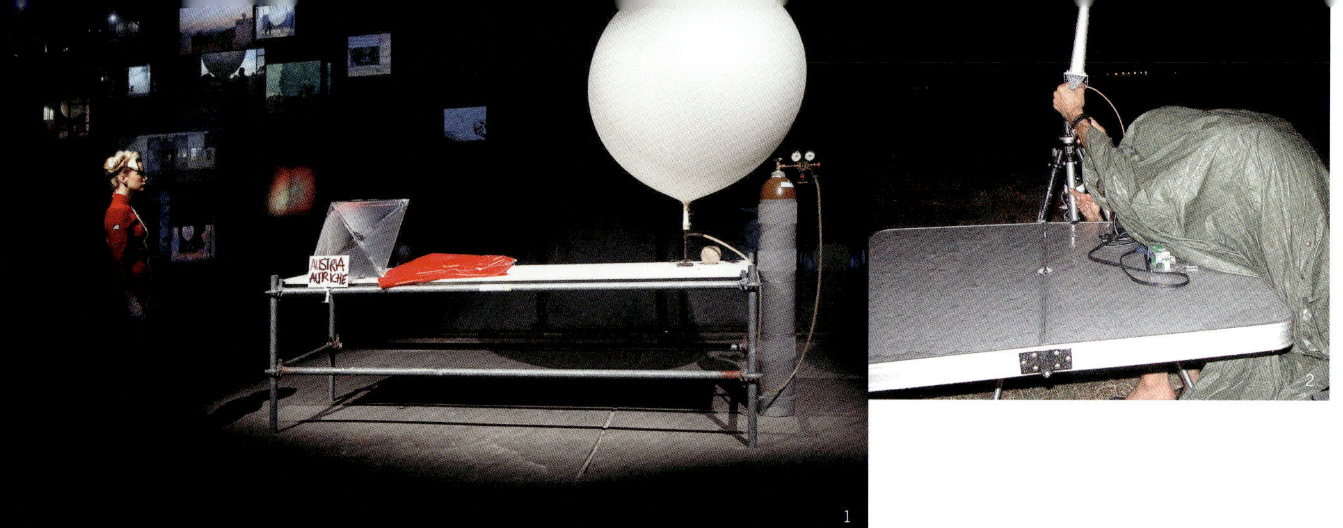

1) *Twelve O'Clock in London: Austria/Autriche,* 2012, performance Kunstraum Dornbirn, photo: Robert Fessler
2) Tracking balloon camera radio signal, Performative Balloon Launch, Nin Brudermann, Venice Biennale
2003, in collaboration with Makrolab and Ministero della Difesa Repubblica Italiana – Servicio Meteorologica,
photo: Makrolab 3) *Twelve O'Clock in London,* 2012, mixed media installation, dim. var., installation view
Kunstraum Dornbirn (details), photos: Robert Fessler

Nin Brudermann
Twelve O'clock in London
249 METROPOLITAN AVE 2nd floor
BROOKLYN NY 112
USA
HUNGARY

1) *Twelve O'Clock in London*, 2012, mixed media installation, dim. var.,
installation view Kunstraum Dornbirn (details), photos: Robert Fessler
2) *Twelve O'Clock in London*, 2010, 7 HD channel video installation TRT
22'00, exhibition view Kunstraum Dornbirn (details), photos: Robert Fessler

Twelve O'Clock in London: Austria/Autriche, 2012, mixed media installation view Kunstraum Dornbirn, photo: Robert Fessler

Diese Ausstellung wurde durch die Mitarbeit der Mitgliedsstaaten der WMO ermöglicht. Mit freundlichem Dank an die Zentralanstalt für Meteorologie und Geodynamik Österreich und an Infocus Technologien für die großzügige Unterstützung.

This exhibition was made possible through the collaboration of the member countries of the WMO, with warm thanks to the Central Institute for Meteorology and Geodynamics Austria and the generous support of Infocus Technologie.

MINISTERIO DE DEFENSA – REPUBLICA ARGENTINA SERVICIO METEOROLOGICO NACIONAL; AUSTRALIAN GOVERNMENT COMMONWEALTH BUREAU OF METEOROLOGY; BUNDESMINISTERIUM FÜR BILDUNG WISSENSCHAFT UND KULTUR ÖSTERREICH – ZENTRALANSTALT FÜR METEOROLOGIE UND GEODYNAMIK; GOVERNMENT OF THE PEOPLE'S REPUBLIC OF BANGLADESH MINISTRY OF DEFENSE – BANGLADESH METEOROLOGICAL DEPARTMENT; BELGIAN FEDERAL SCIENCE POLICY OFFICE – ROYAL METEOROLOGICAL INSTITUTE OF BELGIUM; MINISTRY OF NATURAL RESOURCES AND THE ENVIRONMENT OF BELIZE – BELIZE METEOROLOGICAL SERVICE; MINISTRY OF ENVIRONMENT WILDLIFE AND TOURISM – DEPARTMENT OF METEOROLOGICAL SERVICES REPUBLIC OF BOTSWANA; BRAZIL MINISTERIO DA AGRICULTURA PECUARIA E ABASTECIMENTO – INSTITUTO NACIONAL DE METEOROLOGIA; ENVIRONMENT CANADA – METEOROLOGICAL SERVICE OF CANADA; DIRECCION GENERAL DE AERONAUTICA CIVIL DE CHILE – DIRECCION METEOROLOGICA DE CHILE; STATE COUNCIL OF THE PEOPLE'S REPUBLIC OF CHINA – CHINA METEOROLOGICAL ADMINISTRATION; MINISTRY OF THE ENVIRONMENT OF THE CZECH REPUBLIC – CZECH HYDROMETEOROLOGICAL INSTITUTE; REPUBLIQUE FRANCAISE LE MINISTERE DES TRANSPORTS DE L'EQUIPMENT DU TOURISME ET DE LA MER – METEO FRANCE; BUNDESMINISTERIUM FÜR VERKEHR BAU· UND WOHNUNGSWESEN – DEUTSCHER WETTERDIENST; HELLENIC MINISTRY OF DEFENSE – HELLENIC NATIONAL METEOROLOGICAL SERVICE; COMMERCE AND ECONOMIC DEVELOPMENT BUREAU OF THE GOVERNMENT OF THE HONG KONG SPECIAL ADMINISTRATION – HONG KONG OBSERVATORY; MINISTRY FOR ENVIRONMENT AND WATER – HUNGARIAN METEOROLOGICAL SERVICE; MINISTRY FOR THE ENVIRONMENT – ICELANDIC METEOROLOGICAL OFFICE; INDONESIAN GOVERNMENT AGENCY FOR METEOROLOGY CLIMATOLOGY AND GEOPHYSICS; THE MINISTRY OF ROADS AND TRANSPORTATION OF THE ISLAMIC REPUBLIC OF IRAN – ISLAMIC REPUBLIC OF IRAN METEOROLOGICAL ORGANIZATION; DEPARTMENT OF THE ENVIRONMENT HERITAGE AND LOCAL GOVERNMENT – THE IRISH METEOROLOGICAL SERVICE; MINISTRY OF TRANSPORT OF THE STATE OF ISRAEL – ISRAEL METEOROLOGICAL SERVICE; MINISTERO DELLA DIFESA REPUBBLICA ITALIANA – SERVICIO METEOROLOGICA; MINISTRY OF LAND INFRASTRUCTURE AND TRANSPORT OF JAPAN – JAPAN METEOROLOGICAL AGENCY; MINISTRY OF ENVIRONMENT AND MINERAL RESOURCES – KENYA METEOROLOGICAL DEPARTMENT; LR MINISTRY OF ENVIRONMENT OF THE REPUBLIC OF LATVIA – LATVIAN ENVIRONMENT GEOLOGY AND METEOROLOGY AGENCY; LIBYAN NATIONAL METEOROLOGICAL CENTER – CLIMATE AND AGROMETEOROLOGY DEPARTMENT; MINISTRY OF ENVIRONMENT OF THE REPUBLIC OF LITHUANIA – LITHUANIAN HYDROMETEOROLOGICAL SERVICE; MINISTRY OF TRANSPORT AND PUBLIC WORKS OF THE REPUBLIC OF MALAWI – MALAWI METEOROLOGICAL SERVICES; THE REPUBLIC OF MAURITIUS PRIME MINISTRY – MAURITIUS METEOROLOGICAL SERVICES; SECRETARÍA DE MEDIO AMBIENTE Y RECURSOS NATURALES – MEXICO SERVICIO METEOROLOGICO NACIONAL; MINISTRY OF TRANSPORT PUBLIC WORKS AND WATER MANAGEMENT – THE ROYAL NETHERLANDS METEOROLOGICAL INSTITUTE; NEW ZEALAND MINISTRY OF TRANSPORT – NEW ZEALAND METEOROLOGICAL SERVICE; THE ROYAL NORWEGIAN MINISTRY OF EDUCATION AND RESEARCH – THE NORWEGIAN METEOROLOGICAL INSTITUTE; PAKISTAN MINISTRY OF DEFENSE – PAKISTAN METEOROLOGICAL DEPARTMENT;

EMPRESA DE TRANSMISION ELECTRICA S.A. DE REPUB-
LICA DE PANAMA – HYDROMETEOROLOGY AUTORIDAD
CANAL PANAMA DIVISION DE AMBIENTE; MINISTRY OF
DEFENSE – SERVICIO NACIONAL DE METEOROLOGIA E
HIDROLOGIA DEL PERU; POLAND MINISTRY OF THE EN-
VIRONMENT – THE INSTITUTE OF METEOROLOGY AND
WATER MANAGEMENT; RUSSIAN FEDERAL SERVICE FOR
HYDROMETEOROLOGY AND ENVIRONMENTAL MONITOR-
ING ROSHYDROMET; SEYCHELLES MINISTRY OF THE EN-
VIRONMENT AND NATURAL RESOURCES – NATIONAL ME-
TEOROLOGICAL SERVICES; THE MINISTRY OF ENVIRON-
MENTAL AFFAIRS AND TOURISM OF SOUTH AFRICA –
SOUTH AFRICAN WEATHER SERVICE; MINISTERIO DE ME-
DIO AMBIENTE DE ESPANA – AGENCIA ESTATAL DE METE-
OROLOGIA; MINISTRY OF THE ENVIRONMENT – SWEDISH
METEOROLOGICAL AND HYDROLOGICAL INSTITUTE, EID-
GENÖSSISCHES DEPARTMENT DES INNEREN – FEDERAL
OFFICE OF METEOROLOGY AND CLIMATOLOGY SWITZER-
LAND METEO SUISSE; MINISTRY OF INFORMATION AND
COMMUNICATION TECHNOLOGY – THAI METEOROLOGI-
CAL DEPARTMENT; MINISTRY OF DEFENSE OF THE UNIT-
ED KINGDOM – U.K. METEOROLOGICAL OFFICE; MINISTRY
OF EMERGENCIES AND AFFAIRS OF POPULATION PROTEC-
TION FROM THE CONSEQUENCES OF CHERNOBYL CATAS-
TROPHE OF UKRAINE – UKRAINIAN HYDROMETEORO-
LOGICAL CENTER; UNITED STATES DEPARTMENT OF
COMMERCE – U.S. NATIONAL OCEANIC & ATMOSPHERIC
ADMINISTRATION; REPUBLIC OF UZBEKISTAN HYDROME-
TEOROLOGICAL SERVICE

Twelve O'Clock In London ist ein von der New York Foundation
for the Arts gefördertes Projekt mit finanzieller Unterstützung vom New York State Council on the Arts und von
der Greenwall Foundation.

Twelve O'Clock in London is a sponsored project of the New
York Foundation for the Arts with funding provided by the
New York State Council on the Arts and the Greenwall Foun-
dation New York.

Mit weiterer Unterstützung durch /
With further support from

The Australian Antarctic Division Fellowship for the Arts;
Bundesministerium für Unterricht, Kunst und Kultur, Öster-
reich; Meteo France, TAAF; Direction Régionale Administra-
tive d'Affaires Culturelles, Paris; LE FANAL, Réunion; Min-
istero della Difesa, Repubblica Italiana – Servicio
Meteorologica; La Biennale di Venezia; Italian Air Force –
ReSMA; Makrolab; Commune di Venezia; 4th Floor, New
York; The Norwegian Meteorological Institute; The Royal
Norwegian Ministry of Defense and Armed Forces; NoMad,
Genf; Victoria Hall, Genf; World Meteorological Organiza-
tion, Genf.

Besonderen Dank an / Special thanks to

Carine Richard VanMaele, WMO; Dieter Buchhart; Veronica
Petersen, Lesley Renton, Scott Niesen, InFocus; Natalia
Signoroni, NoMad; Fredrica Jarcho, The Greenwall Founda-
tion, New York; Amanda McDonald Crowley, Eyebeam, New
York; Joanna Lehan; Adam Kleinman; Zan Dumbadze; Tre-
vor Smith; Arfus Greenwood; Sepp R. Brudermann; UAFS,
Salzburg; Institut für Angewandte Forschung, Hochschule
Pforzheim; TVNSP Kansas; Galerie Heike Strelow; Professor
John W. Zillman; Christian Ebner, Permanent Mission of
Austria to the United Nations; Secretary-General of the
United Nations Ban Ki-Moon; Ralf Mayer.

Nin Brudermann

Geboren 1970 in Wien.
Lebt und arbeitet in New York und Wien.
Studium der Philosophie an der Universität
Wien, Studium an der Akademie der bildenden
Künste Wien und an der Schule für künstlerische
Fotografie, Wien. Die Arbeiten Nin Brudermanns,
die als österreichisch-amerikanische Künstlerin
in New York und Wien lebt, sind narrative Recher-
chen, wobei eine Ambiguität zwischen Real und
„Super-Real" besteht.

Born 1970 in Vienna.
Lives and works in New York and Vienna.
Studied philosophy at the University of Vienna,
studied at the Academy of Fine Arts Vienna and
at the Schule für künstlerische Fotografie, Vienna.
The works by Nin Brudermann, who as an
Austrian-American artist lives in New York and
Vienna, are narrative researches, whereby an
ambiguity arises between the real and the
"super real".

**Internationale Stipendien /
International scholarships**
1996–1997 P.S.1 MoMA Contemporary
   Art Center, New York
2003 Fellowship of the Arts, Australian
   Antarctic Division
2006 Arts & Humanities Grant,
   The Greenwall Foundation, New York
2008 Individual Artist Film & Media Grant,
   New York State Council on the Arts,
   fiscal sponsorship of the New York
   Foundation for the Arts
2010 Prix Ars Rothkrebschen (nominated)

**Einzelausstellungen und Screenings (Auswahl) /
Solo exhibitions and screenings (Selection)**
1996 MuseumsQuartier Wien
1997 *Nature Abhors a Naked Singularity*,
   Clocktower Gallery, New York
1998 Galerie Urs Meile (with Christoph Draeger),
   Lucerne
2000 Kunsthalle 8/Kunstbüro, Vienna
2003 Art Chicago Project Space
2004 *NASD Projekt Fledermaus*, Bernsteiner
   Dependance, Vienna
2005 *NASD Projekt Fledermaus*, Priska C. Juschka
   Fine Art, New York
2006 *Animal Stories*, Pianissimo, Milan

2009 *Twelve O'Clock in London*, Victoria Hall,
Geneva
2010 *Late Night Show*, ME Contemporary,
Copenhagen
Twelve O'Clock in London, Kunsthalle Krems
2012 *N.A.B.*, Kunsthallen Nikolaj/
ME Contemporary, Copenhagen

Teilnahme an Gruppenausstellungen (Auswahl) /
Participation in groups shows (Selection)
1993 *Schaulust*, Galerie Hummel, Vienna
1997 P.S.1 Museum, Studio Artist Show, New York,
Kommerzbau, Galerie Bernhard Schindler,
Bern
1998 Independent Film- and Videofestival,
New York
1999 *2–4–6–H* (mit Norman Ohler),
Softmoderne, Berlin
2000 *Circles of Confusion*, Independent Film
Network, Berlin
2001 *Garden Built for You*, Smart Project Space,
Amsterdam
2002 *Cool Times*, Priska C. Juschka Fine Art,
New York
2003 *Attack!*, Kunsthalle Wien,
Space Arts, Maison de la Photographie, Paris,
Twelve O'Clock in London – Station VII,
Makrolab, 50. Venice Biennale

2004 *Handlungsanweisungen*, Kunsthalle Wien
2005 *Space and the Arts*, Yverdon-les-Bains,
Switzerland
BROOKLinVIDEO, Futura Center for
Contemporary Art, Prague
2006 *Switching Worlds – Desires and Identities*,
Austrian Cultural Forum New York
*Zerstörte Welten und die Utopie der
Rekonstruktion*, Kunstraum Dornbirn and
Århus Kunstbygning
2008 *Project One*, ICA Institute of Contemporary
Arts, London und CCA Center of
Contemporary Art, Glasgow
Shifting Values, Austrian Cultural Forum,
Warsaw
Go NYC, Kunsthalle Krems
2009 *Elevator to the Gallows*, Galerie im
Regierungsviertel/Forgotten Bar Project
Berlin at X-Initiative, New York
(with Arfus Greenwood)
2010 *Künstler in der KunstGesellschaft*,
Motorenhalle Dresden
2011 *Dear Thick and Thin*,
ME Contemporary, Copenhagen
2012 *Image Counter Image*, Haus der Kunst
Munich
Twelve O'Clock in London: Austria/Autriche,
Regionale 12, Graz

Anna Karina Hofbauer

Geboren 1973 in Skælskør, Dänemark. Lebt in Wien.
Anna Karina Hofbauer ist Kunsthistorikerin und Freelance-Kuratorin und Autorin mit Schwerpunkt partizipative Kunst von den 1950er Jahren bis zur zeitgenössischen Kunst. Sie studierte in Kopenhagen und Wien. Zu den von ihr kuratierten Ausstellungen gehören u.a. *Making Nature* (Atelier Augarten/Belvedere, Wien, 2002), *Lois & Franziska Weinberger* (Kunsthallen Brandts, Odense, Dänemark, 2004), *Just Use It* (Nordjyllands Kunstmuseum, Aalborg, Dänemark, 2007), *Acting in Utopia* (Landesgalerie Linz, 2007), *Warhol & Basquiat* (Arken Museum of Modern Art, Kopenhagen, 2011, Assistenz Kuratorin).

Born 1973 in Skælskør, Denmark. Lives in Vienna.
Anna Karina Hofbauer is an art historian, a freelance curator and author, with a focus on participative art from the 1950s to the present day. She studied in Copenhagen and Vienna. The exhibitions she curated, among others, are: *Making Nature* (Atelier Augarten/Belvedere, Vienna, 2002), *Lois & Franziska Weinberger* (Kunsthallen Brandts, Odense, Denmark, 2004), *Just Use It* (Nordjyllands Kunstmuseum, Aalborg, Denmark, 2007), *Acting in Utopia* (Landesgalerie Linz, 2007), *Warhol & Basquiat* (Arken Museum of Modern Art, Copenhagen, 2011, assistant curator).

Dieter Buchhart

Dieter Buchhart (1971 geb. in Wien) ist Kurator, Kunsttheoretiker und Künstler. Von 2007 bis Ende 2009 war er Direktor der Kunsthalle Krems. Von 1990 bis 2000 studierte er Biologie und Kunstgeschichte. Er war als Kurator von zahlreichen Ausstellungen in renommierten Institutionen im In- und Ausland. Seit 1999 arbeitet er als Redakteur des *Kunstforum International*. Er ist Autor zahlreicher Monografien, Kataloge und Artikel sowie Interviews u.a. zu Kunst und Wirtschaft. Seine Forschungsschwerpunkte reichen von der Kunst des 19. Jahrhunderts bis zur Gegenwart.

Dieter Buchhart (1971 born in Vienna) is curator, art theorist, artist and from 2007 to the end of 2009 was director of Kunsthalle Krems. 1990–2000 studied biology and art history. Curator of numerous exhibitions in renowned institutions in Austria and abroad Since 1999 senior editor of *Kunstforum International*, and since then responsible for many monographs and interviews, among other things, on art and economic affairs. As an art theorist wrote many articles for catalogues and magazines. His research focus ranges from the art of the 19th century to the present day.

Dokumentation zur Ausstellung
Documentation of the exhibition

Nin Brudermann
Twelve O'Clock In London: Austria/Autriche
22. Juni – 19. August 2012

Ausstellung / Exhibition:
Montagehalle, Jahngasse 9
Büro / Office: Marktstraße 33,
A-6850 Dornbirn
Tel 0043-(0)5572-55044
Fax 0043-(0)5572-55044 4838
kunstraum@dornbirn.at,
www.kunstraumdornbirn.at

Ausstellung / Exhibition
Kuratorin der Ausstellung / Curator of
the Exhibition:
Anna Karina Hofbauer, Wien / Vienna
Organisation, Produktion / Organisation,
Production: Hans Dünser
Videodokumentation / Video Documentation:
Hans Jörg Kapeller

Kunstraum Dornbirn
Präsident / President: Ekkehard Bechtold
Leitung / Direction: Hans Dünser
PR / Marketing: Herta Pümpel
Sekretariat / Secretariat: Karin Dünser

Katalog / Catalog
Herausgeber / Editor:
Kunstraum Dornbirn, Hans Dünser;
Anna Karina Hofbauer, Wien / Vienna
Gestaltung / Grafic Design:
Flax, Jutz, Mätzler Agentur für Kommunikation
Redaktion / Editing:
Herta Pümpel
Lektorat / Proofreading:
Verlag für moderne Kunst Nürnberg
Texte / Texts:
Anna Karina Hofbauer, Dieter Buchhart
Übersetzung / Translation:
Jeanne Haunschild, Bonn

Fotonachweis / Photo credits
© Fessler Fotografie, Robert Fessler,
6923 Lauterach, Österreich / Austria

Schrift / Typeface:
News Gothic Regular / Italic / Bold
Papier / Paper:
Gemini weiß 300 g/qm,
Gmund Colors 300 g/qm, Clarobulk 150 g/qm
Druck / Print:
Buchdruckerei Lustenau GmbH, Millenium Park 10,
6890 Lustenau, Österreich / Austria

© Nürnberg 2012, Kunstraum Dornbirn,
Nin Brudermann, Verlag für moderne Kunst
Nürnberg und die Autoren / and the authors

Alle Rechte vorbehalten / All Rights reserved

Printed in Austria
ISBN 978-3-86984-363-6

Bibliografische Information
Der Deutschen Nationalbibliothek
Die Deutsche Nationalbibliothek verzeichnet diese
Publikation in der Deutschen Nationalbibliografie;
detaillierte bibliografische Daten sind im Internet
über http://dnb.ddb.de abrufbar.

Bibliographic Information published by
Die Deutsche Nationalbibliothek
Die Deutsche Nationalbibliothek lists this
publication in the Deutschen Nationalbibliografie;
detailed bibliographic data is available in the
Internet at http://dnb.ddb.de

Distributed outside Europe
D.A.P. / Distributed Art Publishers, Inc.
155 Sixth Avenue, 2nd Floor, New York, NY 100
phone 001-(0)212-627 19 99,
fax 001-(0)212-627 94 84

Distributed in the United Kingdom
Cornerhouse Publications; 70 Oxford Street,
Manchester M 1 5 NH, UK
phone 0044-(0)161-200 15 03,
fax 0044-(0)161-200 15 04

Dank an die Autoren / Our thanks to the authors:
Anna Karina Hofbauer, Wien / Vienna
Dieter Buchhart, Wien / Vienna

Mit freundlicher Unterstützung / Thanks to:
Der Subventionsgeber:
Stadt Dornbirn, Land Vorarlberg und Republik
Österreich – bm:ukk, Kunstsektion.

Des Hauptsponsors des Kunstraum Dornbirn,
der Dornbirner Sparkasse Bank AG.

**Lois und Franziska
Weinberger**
Wir sind des Baumes müde
32 S./pp.
Deutsch/English
ISBN 978-3-936711-26-4

Gloria Friedmann
Play-Back aus Eden
36 S./pp.
Deutsch/English
ISBN 978-3-936711-83-7

Teres Wydler
*N.I.C.E –
Nature in Corrosive Ecstasy©*
60 S./pp.
Deutsch/English
ISBN 978-3-939738-68-8

Tamara Grcic
lichtgrün, grün, feuille-morte
32 S./pp.
Deutsch/English
ISBN 978-3-936711-38-7

*Zerstörte Welten
und die Utopie der
Rekonstruktion*
108 S./pp.
Deutsch/English
ISBN 978-3-938821-74-9

Urs-P. Twellmann
Forstrevier 3
32 S./pp.
Deutsch/English
ISBN 978-3-939738-67-1

Tony Matelli
Fuck'd and The Oracle
40 S./pp.
Deutsch/English
ISBN 978-3-936711-57-8

Simon Wachsmuth
*die Dinge kann ich
nicht mehr sehn,
wie ich sie einmal sah*
32 S./pp.
Deutsch/English
ISBN 978-3-939738-13-8

Mark Dion
Concerning Hunting
160 S./pp.
English/Deutsch
ISBN 978-3775721974

Franz Huemer
*... der letze Rest vom
abgespaltenen Paradies*
36 S./pp.
Deutsch/English
ISBN 978-3-936711-76-9

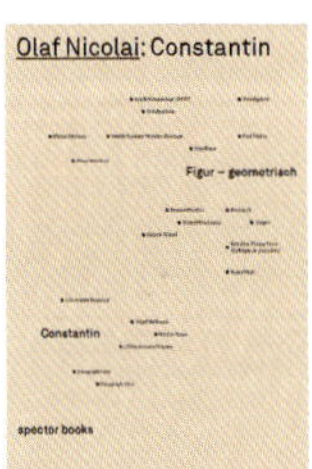

Olaf Nicolai
Constantin
Künstlerbuch
28 S./pp.
Deutsch/English/Français
ISBN 978-3940064813

Simon Starling
Plant Room
32 S./pp.
Deutsch/English
ISBN 978-3-940748-75-1

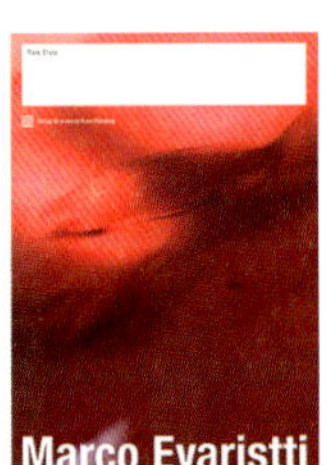

Marco Evaristti
Pink State
40 S./pp.
Deutsch/English
ISBN 978-3-936711-82-0

Michel Blazy
Falling Garden
32 S./pp.
Deutsch/English
ISBN 978-3-939738-50-3

Roman Signer
Installation
Unfall als Skulptur
40 S./pp.
Deutsch/English
ISBN 978-3-940748-74-4

Igor Sacharow-Ross
Nicht gefiltert
60 S./pp.
Deutsch/English
ISBN 978-3-941185-83-8

Peter Buggenhout
caterpillar logic
60 S./pp.
Deutsch/English
ISBN 978-3-86984-133-5

Nin Brudermann
Twelve O'Clock In London:
Austria/Autriche
60 S./pp.
Deutsch/English
ISBN 978-3-86984-363-6

Fides Becker
Ein Panorama
60 S./pp.
Deutsch/English
ISBN 978-3-941185-70-8

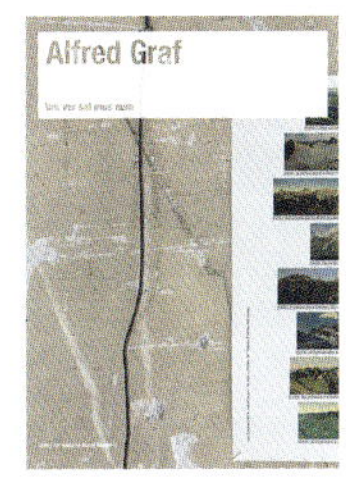

Alfred Graf
Uni ver sal mus eum
60 S./pp.
Deutsch/English
ISBN 978-3-86984-243-1

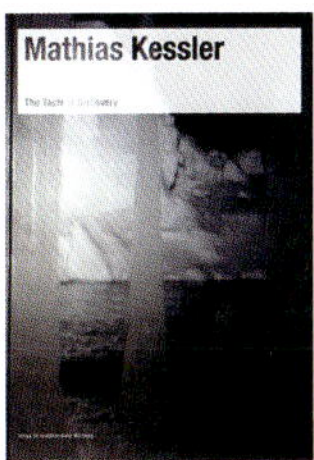

Mathias Kessler
The Taste of Discovery
60 S./pp.
Deutsch/English
ISBN 978-3-941185-71-5

Erwin Wurm
Narrow House
60 S./pp.
Deutsch/English
ISBN 978-3-86984-245-5

Jan Kopp
Das endlose Spiel –
Le jeu sans fin
60 S./pp.
Deutsch/English/Français
ISBN 978-3-86984-030-7

Didier Marcel
Red Harvest
64 S./pp.
Deutsch/English/Français
ISBN 978-3-86984-247-9

Klaus Mosettig
Nature morte
144 S./pp.
Deutsch/English
ISBN 978-3-86984-028-4

Not Vital
Lasst hundert Blumen
blühen
48 S./pp.
Deutsch/English
ISBN 978-3-86984-348-3